I0292602

Marta Pallavidini

(A)synchronic (Re)actions

CHRONOI

Zeit, Zeitempfinden, Zeitordnungen
Time, Time Awareness, Time Management

Edited by
Eva Cancik-Kirschbaum, Christoph Markschies and
Hermann Parzinger

on behalf of the Einstein Center Chronoi

Volume 14

Marta Pallavidini

(A)synchronic (Re)actions

Crises and Their Perception in Hittite History

DE GRUYTER

EINSTEIN CENTER Chronoi

ISBN 978-3-11-171212-3
e-ISBN (PDF) 978-3-11-171238-3
e-ISBN (EPUB) 978-3-11-171258-1
ISSN 2701-1453
DOI https://doi.org/10.1515/9783111712383

Library of Congress Control Number: 2025931575

Bibliographic information published by the Deutsche Nationalbibliothek
The Deutsche Nationalbibliothek lists this publication in the Deutsche Nationalbibliografie; detailed bibliographic data are available on the internet at http://dnb.dnb.de.

www.degruyter.com
Questions about General Product Safety Regulation:
productsafety@degruyterbrill.com

To Minerva

Before reaching the final line, however, he had already understood that he would never leave that room,
for it was foreseen that the city of mirrors (or mirages)
would be wiped out by the wind
and exiled from the memory of men at the precise moment when Aureliano Babilonia would finish deciphering the parchments, and that everything written on them was unrepeatable since time immemorial and forever more, because races condemned to one hundred years of solitude did not have a second opportunity on earth

(Gabriel García Márquez, *One Hundred Years of Solitude*, translation by G. Rabassa)

Acknowledgments

I would like to express my deepest gratitude to all those who have supported and guided me throughout the process of writing this book. Though it may be small, it has certainly been a long journey.

First and foremost, I am profoundly grateful to the Einstein Center Chronoi Executive Board for having welcomed me as a research fellow and for having supported my research project *(A)synchronic (re)actions: Crises and Their Potential in Hittite History*. The year spent at the EC-Chronoi provided fruitful academic exchanges as well as the quiet time needed to engage in this challenging and stimulating project.

I also want to express my gratitude to the EC-Chronoi Team for having provided resources, support, and access to crucial research materials. Their assistance has been key to enabling the completion of this book by helping me meet my deadlines and expectations for this publication. They made me feel at home.

I would like to thank my colleagues at the EC-Chronoi who have shared their wisdom, insights, and expertise. Their encouragement and constructive feedback were invaluable, helping me refine and deepen my understanding of something as volatile as the concept and perception of time.

I would like to express my gratitude to the proofreader for having done a wonderful job correcting my English and to the reviewer for having taken the time to read and review my manuscript.

To my husband Marco, my daughter Minerva, and my closest friends, whose unwavering love, patience, and understanding gave me the emotional strength to persevere through a long year of research and a hectic summer of writing—thank you for being my timeless foundation.

Berlin, January 2025

Foreword

When researching antiquity, or history in general, time is always a fundamental and yet tricky concept. Time is, in fact, the unit of measurement of the distance between us and the culture(s) that we study, and the misuse of this concept can lead – as has happened in the past and still happens today – to misinterpretations of the historical events in the best case or even, in the worst-case scenario, to the evaluation of history through our own contemporary *Weltanschauung*. Time is, therefore, in the historical perspective, a matter of perception and perspective.

We must ask ourselves: what is our perception of the past events? What was the perception of the people who lived at the time of these events? Did all the actors involved have the same perception (and awareness) of contemporary events?

Time is, therefore, an essential element of the work of the historian, not only as a key factor in the study of chronologies, sequences, and periodizations, but also in the more complex question of whether the perceptions of and perspectives on events differ from actor to actor, not only between modern researchers and the ancient culture(s), but also among ancient actors as well.

Dealing with this idea of time within the historical perspective is challenging, since the reconstruction of the events themselves and, even more so, of their perception is based on available sources that are partial in two senses: first, they are not complete, since even the best-preserved set of sources (written and/or material) contains some missing pieces; second, they represent an inherently biased point of view, specifically the one of the culture that produced the sources. Even in the best-case scenario in which different sources from different cultures that inform on the same events have survived, it is impossible to reconstruct a perfectly objective narrative of the events described.

The partiality of the sources is even more difficult when investigating the topic of crisis, as is the case for the present study.

This book aims to study the perception of crises in Hittite Anatolia (ca. 1650 – 1180 BCE) from three different perspectives by interpreting data gleaned from the available written sources. The first perspective that will be examined is that of the Hittites, the second is of the neighboring countries, and the third is our own perspective as historians.

Two fundamental concepts are necessary for this study, therefore they will be discussed in the introduction: the first is the concept of crisis, and the second is the concept of (a)synchronicity. As mentioned before, time is a crucial concept in the study of Antiquity, since crises are not always perceived synchronically. For example, when we compare the perspective of the Hittites and that of their neighboring countries, we would expect their records to reflect a similar perception of the exis-

 https://doi.org/10.1515/9783111712383-002

tence of a crisis, since the two actors are coeval – or to use a catchier expression – share the same temporal frame. However, this expected synchronicity cannot always be taken for granted. It will be shown that in some of the case studies presented in the next chapters, the perception of a crisis is asynchronic even when the cultures exist within the same temporal frame. From the perspective of the historian, asynchronicity is at work, since our temporal frame is greatly removed from that of the ancient actors, yet if we rely on and correctly interpret the sources available to us, it becomes clear that we might perceive a crisis in Hittite Anatolia more synchronically than might be expected. Finally, even the perception of the Hittites could be – at the same time – asynchronic and synchronic, since it is possible that they misinterpreted the signs of an actual crisis as it unfolded and perceived it as a crisis only after it took place or even after it ended. According to the definitions of crisis that will be discussed in the next chapter, and together with the concept of (a)synchronicity, the book will consider four case studies that will be presented and discussed in the second chapter: the transition from the Old to the Middle Hittite kingdom; the Battle of Qadesh; the reign of Ḫattušili III; and finally, the fall of the Hittite Empire. The third and final chapter of the book will deal with the interpretation of the data: the ultimate goal is to re-define crises in Hittite Anatolia using the temporality of the (a)synchronic perception of crises as a crucial factor in the evaluation and interpretation of the historical events.

Contents

Acknowledgments — IX

Foreword — XI

1 Introduction: Crisis, (A)synchronicity, and the Hittites — 1
1.1 Crisis — **1**
1.2 (A)synchronicity — **3**
1.3 The Hittites — **7**
1.3.1 A Word on Periodization — **10**
1.4 The Case Studies — **14**

2 The Case Studies — 17
2.1 Case Study #1 The Proclamation of Telipinu: Misleading Perceptions — **17**
2.1.1 Why the Proclamation of Telipinu? — **17**
2.1.2 The Text — **18**
2.1.3 A Recurring Crisis — **21**
2.1.4 Misleading Perception — **22**
2.2 Case Study #2 The Battle of Qadesh: Asynchronicity at Work — **24**
2.2.1 Preliminary Remarks — **24**
2.2.2 The Sources — **26**
2.2.3 The Unfolding of the Hittite-Egyptian Relations — **32**
2.2.4 Asynchronicity at Work — **34**
2.3 Case Study #3 The Reign of Ḫattušili III: A Crisis in (Temporal) Disguise — **37**
2.3.1 The Milestones of Ḫattušili's Career — **37**
2.3.2 The Sources — **39**
2.3.3 The Crisis (or Crises) — **41**
2.3.4 Asynchronicity in Disguise — **46**
2.4 Case Study #4 The End of the Hittite Empire: Asynchronic Synchronicity — **47**
2.4.1 The End of an Era — **47**
2.4.2 The Sources — **50**
2.4.3 Asynchronic Synchronicity — **56**

3 Conclusions: Asynchonicity and (Re)-interpretation of Crises — 58
3.1 Crisis: Temporality vs Perception — **58**
3.2 Re-interpreting Crisis in Hittite History — **60**

1 Introduction: Crisis, (A)synchronicity, and the Hittites

1.1 Crisis

The term "crisis" seems to be, at least in the contemporary world, not only overused in a variety of contexts but also assuming very different nuances of meaning. For instance, it is "personal crisis", "financial crisis", "political crisis", "environmental crisis", "psychological crisis" and so on, meaning the word crisis is very general and related to many diverse topics and contexts.

This is not a surprise, since the word "crisis" does not have a single precise definition. When we observe the definitions attested in only one dictionary – for instance, the *Cambridge Dictionary* – we learn that crisis is defined as "a time of great disagreement, confusion, or suffering" but also as "an extremely difficult or dangerous point in a situation", and again "a moment during a serious illness when there is the possibility of suddenly getting either better or worse".[1] The common denominators are the negativity of the situation and the fact that an action is necessary in order to change the critical status. The fact that there are so many meanings contained within this polysemic word is explained by the fact that the ancient Greek κρίσις (krisis) derives from the verb κρίνειν, which also has a variety of meanings: "to separate, to divide, to distinguish, to order, to decide".[2] Even if the Greek term was originally employed in specific disciplines, such as medicine or theology, from the 17th century CE on, the term became common in reference to politics, economics, and psychology, as well as in other fields, such as history and archaeology where the term is still used without regard for precise meaning. In a very general fashion, it is possible to say that the term "crisis" describes a point in time that "separates" a before and an after, as in the original meaning of the Greek verb.[3]

It is already clear from the meaning(s) of crisis that the concept is strictly related to the idea of time. In fact, not only does a crisis separate a before and an after (not necessarily with a radical change) but it is also always linked to a momentous situation in which something meaningful happens, or with a specific moment in time in which a decision has to be made, or when the culmination of previous events finds its resolution at a precise point in time or becomes manifest.

1 https://dictionary.cambridge.org/dictionary/english/crisis (last access 27/01/2025).

2 https://en.wiktionary.org/wiki/κρίνω (last access 27/01/2025).

3 See Koselleck 2006.

 https://doi.org/10.1515/9783111712383-003

It is clear that there are very few suitable theoretical approaches to investigating crises in history, particularly ancient history. For instance, J. Rüsen identifies three types of crises: 1. "Normal" crises, 2. "Critical" crises, and 3. "Catastrophic" crises. Normal crises can be dealt with through the application of known patterns, and they do not necessarily result in a change. Critical crises presuppose adjustments or changes in order to be overcome. Catastrophic crises usually have traumatic consequences, and they lead to a change in the existing patterns. In Rüsen's view, the focus is not on the crisis itself, but on how it is handled. In particular, the central question is whether it is possible to overcome a crisis by reverting to existing patterns of interpretation: the more this is impossible, the more catastrophic the crisis.[4]

This approach to crisis in historical contexts can of course be applied to our study, but it lacks two fundamental elements: the first is that the focus of my study is (a)synchronic perceptions of the crises themselves and not on the resources and meaning used to overcome them. The second is that the concept of time (both the concept in general and also the perception of its meaning) is tightly intertwined with the definition of crisis.

Therefore, since the goal is to consider the element of time as related to the concept of crisis, the most suitable approach is, in my opinion, the one taken by R. Koselleck.[5]

Koselleck attempted to define the meaning of the word crisis in relation to its use throughout history. In order to do this, he proposed four different definitions for crisis, each related to the element of time that is crucial to the present study. According to his definition, crisis can be defined in four different ways: 1) "a chain of events leading to a culminating, decisive point at which action is required", 2) "a unique and final point", 3) "a permanent or conditional category pointing to a critical situation which may constantly recur or else to situations in which decisions have momentous consequences", 4) "a historically immanent transitional phase".[6]

These definitions are superbly useful for the present study, because in them the concept of time is related to all four definitions of crisis: in terms of a specific moment in the first two definitions, and as a time span (whether recurring cyclically or only occasionally) in the other two. Furthermore, in all of these definitions time is crucial also in linking the three chronological stages of the crisis: antecedent events, the crisis itself, and its aftermath. The definition that will be used in this study is, therefore, a working definition (or working definitions) of crisis. The advantage of

---

4 Rüsen 2013, 49–51; Rüsen 2020, 63–65.

5 It goes without saying that the work of R. Koselleck has been controversial in the past and still is today. The scope of this study, however, does not purpose a review of the work of Koselleck, but instead intends to find the best fit approach for a discussion of crisis with a focus on temporality.

6 Koselleck 2006, 371–372.

this approach is two-fold: first, it already addresses time and its attendant difficulties, such as multitemporality and (a)synchronicity; and second, it allows the possibility of considering different types of case studies with two common denominators, namely, crisis and temporality with their specific interpretative nuances.

1.2 (A)synchronicity

The use and the understanding of the term "crisis" is not the only complex issue in the present study, indeed, the same can also be said about the concept of (a)synchronicity.

In order to clarify the use and meaning of the concept of (a)synchronicity in this work, it is necessary to first define other concepts that are intertwined with the idea of (a)synchronicity, such as (multi)temporality, chronology, and periodization[7]. The starting point is the verb "to synchronize", whose basic meaning is "to occur at the same time", or as is well-defined by H. Jordheim, "to synchronize refers to actions or activities that cause something to happen together, coincide, to occur or to unfold at the same time".[8]

The term "synchronization" comes from the most basic meaning of the verb "to synchronize", whose usage in everyday life is also mostly unproblematic and can refer to the activity of synchronizing watches or agendas. On a broader scale, synchronicity can refer to the introduction of the same calendar in different parts of the world or of Greenwich Mean Time.[9] The concept of synchronization becomes much more complicated and controversial when it is used in relation to history and historiography. For example, E. Alvater and B. Mahnkopf describe synchronization as when "the plurality of times in the plurality of world regions are drawn together to one single standardized and standardizing world time".[10] The resulting consequence of this description is on the one hand a linear idea of history – one that was already diffused throughout the world in the nineteenth century albeit in different terms – and, on the other hand, the idea that there is one time frame in which all history unfolds.

However, the idea that history has one time, one speed, and one rhythm can be invalidated by the quite simple observation that history is not in sync, and, more specifically, with increasing questioning of the idea of progress itself. This does not mean, of course, that some events are not coeval, and the importance of building

7 On periodization see specifically Ch. 3.1.
8 Jordheim 2017, 59.
9 Jordheim 2017.
10 Altvater / Mahnkopf 1996, 21.

chronologies especially in ancient history is a fundamental practice to help disentangle issues related to the sequences of kings, coeval events in different places, material culture, and so on. Nonetheless, chronologies can also raise issues, especially in the field of archaeology, as pointed out by G. Lucas, according to whom "chronology – whether relative or absolute – is theoretically problematic and for one chief reason: it presents time as a uniform, linear phenomenon."[11] He goes on to argue that processes, including archaeological ones, which operate on different time scales require different approaches, meaning that he finds nonsynchronicity in archaeology as well as in other processes, therefore necessitating careful consideration of this issue in archaeological research.

What he means by the nonsynchronicity of history is that "elements, words, concepts, institutional structures, or social and political practices" feature "duration, narrative structures, visions of the future and dreams of the past, rhythms, continuities and discontinuities" in different fashions.[12]

History is, therefore, not squeezed in one single temporality but rather unfolds in different temporal frameworks or, in other words, history is multitemporal. There is no univocal definition of multitemporality, rather the purpose of the concept is to create a theoretical and methodological tool that can refine the understanding of history from a linear progressive succession of events to a multifaceted combination of factors.

We can define multitemporality as did G. Gurvitch with his eight types of time, all of which are connected with social manifestation[13], or we could define it as the braudelian variation between the events, the cycles of the economic and social structures, and the *longue durée.*[14] Alternatively, multitemporality can also be interpreted as the concept of *Ungleichzeitigkeit* (nonsynchronicity) of R. Koselleck, i. e. moments of nonsychronicity in a specific historical period.[15] These examples demonstrate that multitemporality can be used as a working tool for historians[16] and that it is still a roadmap for interpretation, even though it is not a universally established working framework. Despite this limitation, two elements can be drawn from the concept of multitemporality: first, nonsynchronicity (or asynchronicity) is – to some degree – always present in historical time; second, since asynchronicity characterizes each historical period, we can argue that it also characterizes each historical moment.

11 Lucas 2005, 10.
12 Jordheim 2017, 66.
13 Gurvitch 1958.
14 Braudel 1958.
15 Koselleck 2000.
16 For a more in-depth analysis and a general state of the field see Jordheim 2014.

These elements have a significant implication for this study, specifically that asynchronicity must be at work – at least in theory – in each case study.

Having discussed synchronicity and temporality, it is necessary to bring this study into the picture and, consequently, to slightly switch perspective once again. The three perspectives that are taken into consideration, namely that of of the Hittites, the one of the neighboring countries, and ours as historians can be thought of as three separate mathematical sets (see Fig. 1), each of which has its own perspective on and interpretation of the crises.

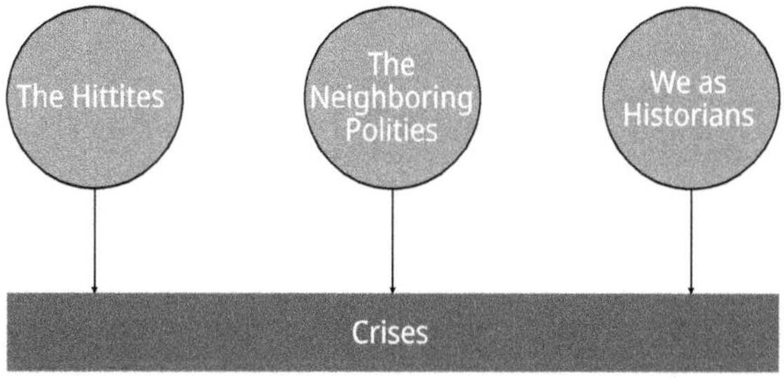

Fig. 1: Scheme of the connection between crises and the three perspectives.

If we add the dimension of temporality, without any implication yet concerning either (a)synchronicity or any theory of multitemporality, the perspective of the Hittites and that of their neighboring countries are included in a single set, and our perspectives as historians are in a different set, since we exist in a different temporality (Fig. 2).

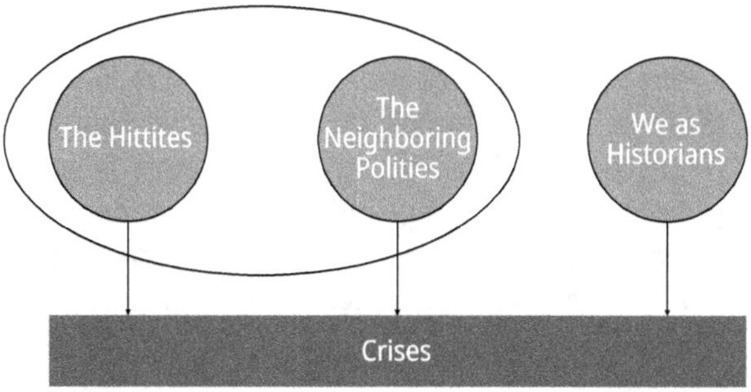

Fig. 2: Scheme of the relations between the perspectives #1.

These schemes are, of course, fairly intuitive, indeed we could even say they are only common sense. However, things change when one further dimension comes into play, namely, multitemporality, which can be schematically represented as follows (Fig. 3):

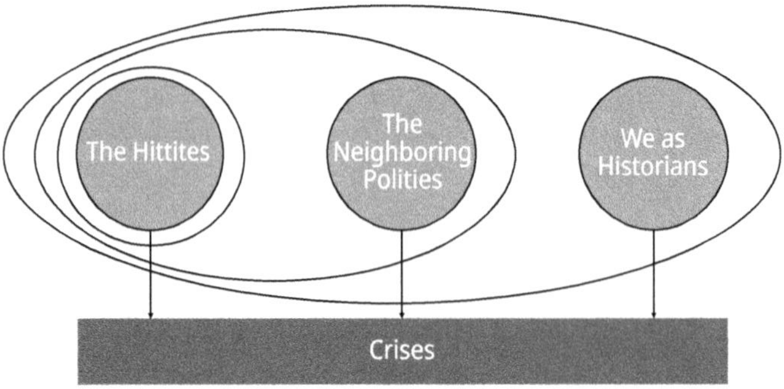

Fig. 3: Scheme of the relations between the perspectives #2.

Now three different temporalities can be detected, which are, however, not necessarily distinct from one another.

Within the first temporality, that of the Hittites, each event or series of events also has its own temporality. The second temporality is the one of the "regional system" (or "oligopoly") that has its own rhythm, structures, continuities, and discontinuities. As M. Liverani defines it:

> A king who cannot officially pretend to be the only ruler in a universe of subject, nevertheless does not necessarily considers everyone to be his equal. There remains a hierarchy in plurality, the result of a determination on the part of the powers to keep the partial, regional centrality that they have already attained. In this situation, an "oligopoly" arrangement is best suited to the interests of its members.[17]

In other words, the system is organized as a "Great Powers' Club"[18], each with a regional center, i.e. Egypt, Hittite Anatolia, Babylonia, Assyria, Mittani, Aḫḫiyawa, and some subordinate polities that depended on one of the Great Powers. Since the Hittites were part of the regional system, their temporality partially overlaps or is at least tangent to that of the system, if, however, not completely superimposable.

The third temporality, ours as historians, has different features but also includes the other two temporalities.

The final element to be considered is the question of where (a)synchronicity comes from. Two factors are crucial in answering this question: the sources and

17 Liverani 2001, 39.
18 Liverani 2000.

the multitemporalities themselves. As already mentioned, the sources are not, of course, complete, and it is also safe to say that none of the actors involved (including us as historians) had access to the totality of the sources available. Therefore, access to a different subset of sources represents a first cause of asynchronicity. Second, the existence of three different temporalities with partially different rhythms, structures, and narratives causes an asynchronic perception of the events, like three concentric spheres each moving in overlapping orbits at a different pace, synchronizing only partially and from time to time.

1.3 The Hittites

It is of course beyond the purpose of this study to give an in-depth description of Hittite culture and history, but in order to better understand the considerations that are part of the case studies, it is in my opinion necessary to set some coordinates.[19]

Hittite culture flourished in Anatolia between the 17th and the end of the 13th/beginning of the 12th century BCE (End of the Middle Age and Late Bronze Age) and had its center – at least as far it is possible to reconstruct from the written sources – in the capital city of Ḫattuša (modern-day Boğazkale).

Since the first excavation campaigns in the early 20th century, archaeologists have found about 30,000 written clay[20] tablets and fragments, which have provided profound insights into Hittite culture.

The texts belong to different genres, specifically: cultic texts (rituals, descriptions of festivals, prayers), legal texts (treaties, decrees, edicts, court records, instructions and oaths, and land donations), letters, omens and oracles, literary texts and myths, school texts, administrative texts (*inter alia* cult inventories, text catalogues), and historiographic texts.[21]

19 The most updated collected work on the topic is de Martino (ed.) 2022.

20 Concerning the material on which the documents were written, there are significant exceptions: first, it is *communis opinio* that many documents were written on a support that has not been preserved (see Marazzi 1994, Waal 2011, Cammarosano *et al.* 2019); second, among the written sources there is the so-called Bronze Tablet, a treaty between the Hittite king Tutḫaliya IV and his cousin Kurunta, king of Tarḫuntašša, written on bronze. Some documents mention other metals as support for the writing of documents, like silver and gold (for silver tablets see CTH 91, obv 1–3; for the reference to a gold tablet see CTH 50, left edge 6; for reference to an iron tablet see CTH 106.II.2, obv. 21).

21 For a complete overview the reference work is still the *Catalogue des textes Hittites* by E. Laroche, first published in 1971, and now also available online: http://www.hethport.uni-wuerzburg.de/CTH (last access 27/01/2025).

The Hittite written sources offer a rich tapestry composed of the complex interplay of powerful societal and cultural forces in a multicultural and multilingual environment.[22] The complexity of this situation is reflected in the fact that several different languages are attested in the texts. In fact, since the beginning of Hittitology, scholars have been able to identify several different languages in the Hittite written sources: Hittite, Luwian, Palaic (all three being Indo-European languages), Akkadian (Semitic), Sumerian, Hurrian, and Hattic (the linguistic group to which the last three languages belong is still debated).[23] Not all of these languages are attested at the same frequency in the texts. The majority of them are written in Hittite, but Akkadian and Hurrian are also well-attested, while the other languages are much less common.

Thanks to the written documentation from Ḫattuša, as well as from other sites inside and outside Hittite Anatolia, it has been possible to reconstruct the sequence of the Hittite kings (s. Fig. 4)[24]. However, while the succession of the Hittite kings is still partially debatable, especially for the phase that precedes the beginning of the archives in Ḫattuša,[25] the list of the kings from Ḫattušili I, the first king undoubtedly documented in the texts, to Šuppiluliuma II, the last king known from the sources, it is quite certain.

Old Kingdom	**Middle Kingdom**	**Empire**
Ḫuzziya (I) (?)	Alluwamna	Šuppiluliuma I
Labarna (?)	Ḫantili II	Arnuwanda II
Ḫattušili I	Taḫurwaili	Muršili II
Muršili I	Zidanta II	Muwatalli II
Ḫantili I	Ḫuzziya II	Muršili III (Urḫi-Teššup)
Zidanta I	Muwatalli I	Ḫattušili III
Ammuna	**(Early Empire)**	Tutḫaliya IV
Ḫuzziya II	Tutḫaliya I/II	Arnuwanda III
Telipinu	Arnuwanda I	Šuppiluliuma II
	Tutḫaliya III	

Fig. 4: Chart of the Hittite kings and of the periodization of Hittite History.

Therefore, we have an accurate, albeit general, succession list of the Hittite kings.

22 On the linguistic contacts see most recently Giusfredi *et al.* 2023.

23 On the newly discovered language, Kalasmaic, see https://www.uni-wuerzburg.de/en/news-and-events/news/detail/news/new-indo-european-language-discovered (last access 27/01/2025).

24 On this periodization see Ch. 1.3.1.

25 Extensively on the topic see recently Klinger 2022 and van den Hout 2021, 38–56.

However, for the purposes of this study, two further aspects of Hittite history and culture should be mentioned. The first concerns the state of the documentation, in particular its dating. The majority of the documents date to the last period of the Hittite history, the so-called Empire Period, and their language is marked by researchers as "junghethitisch" (New Hittite) or "spätjunghethitisch" (Late New Hittite).[26] A significant number of texts labelled as "jh" or "sjh" are copies or revised versions of older documents.[27] However, the number of actual documents dated to the Old or the Middle Kingdom ("althethitisch" – Old Hittite and "mittelhethitisch"- Middle Hittite) is relatively small in comparison to the later texts.[28] Since this study of crises and their perception in Hittite Anatolia is based on the written sources, this distribution of texts by date must be kept in mind since it may influence – at least in part – our interpretation and evaluation of the case studies.

The second aspect is strictly historical and is related to the international sphere of influence of the Hittite polity. In fact, the period of the "Great Powers'Club",[29] i. e. the international society of the Great Kings, independent monarchs[30] who controlled subordinated polities, began only with the reign of Šuppiluliuma I – also when the Empire period began – and continued until the end of the written sources from Ḫattuša during the reign of Šuppiluliuma II. During the 14th and 13th century BCE the Great Kings were in constant contact in the form of letters written in cuneiform, usually in Akkadian, on clay tablets, as well as with goods and people.[31] Therefore, in this period the international connections were closer and better documented than in the previous periods of the Hittite history, which allows

26 See S. Košak, hethiter.net: hetkonk (2.plus): https://www.hethport.uni-wuerzburg.de/hetkonk/hetkonk_abfrageF.php (last access 27/01/2025). For a recent contribution on the dating of the texts with paleography see Klinger 2022 with the discussion of the previous literature.

27 The *Chicago Hittite Dictionary* distinguishes between language and script, when a text shows a discrepancy between the two.

28 See S. Košak, hethiter.net: hetkonk (2.plus): https://www.hethport.uni-wuerzburg.de/hetkonk/hetkonk_abfrageF.php (last access 27/01/2025).

29 Liverani 2000.

30 These monarchs are the Hittite king, the Egyptian pharaoh, the king of Babylonia, the king of Mittani (until its conquest by Šuppiluliuma I), the king of Assyria (from a later point in time) and the king of Aḫḫiyawa (for a short period). Subordinate to Ḫatti were Ugarit, Amurru, Nuḫašše, Aleppo, Karkemiš, and Tarḫuntašša as well as the Arzawa-polities such as Mira-Kuwaliya, the Šeḫa-River-Land, Ḫapalla and Wiluša, and other Anatolian territories like Ḫayaša. Not all these polities were subordinated to Ḫatti for the whole Empire period, but with these polities the subordination was ratified by means of a treaty, in which the Hittite kings established the conditions of the subordination and, more generally, of the relation between them and the subordinate polities.

31 See Zaccagnini 1973 and 1990.

historians to explore the international situation through multiple perspectives, not only that of the Hittites.

If the first aspect, the chronological origination of the sources, especially affects our own perception of the Hittite crises as historians and supports our exploration of the perspective of the Hittites themselves, the second aspect, namely the preservation of documents from multiple contemporary cultures and polities, also helps shape our understanding of the crises as perceived by the peoples surrounding the Hittites, since they share a common infosphere.[32] The richness of sources is of course always an advantage for interpretation by the historian, however, it has to be underlined that richness of source does not necessarily mean their uniform distribution, meaning that some perspectives may remain inaccessible because they are not represented in the documentation, resulting in an incomplete picture of the multiplicity of perspectives on a crisis.

1.3.1 A Word on Periodization

Since historians like Marc Bloch[33] and Jacques Le Goff[34] underlined the interconnection between time and history, it became clear that periodization is an intrinsic concept when dealing with history.

As mentioned in the earlier discussion of the concepts of (a)synchronicity and multitemporalities in section 1.2, the idea of periodization presents three significant characteristics. First, it is conventional, meaning that it is – at least most of the time – not related to dates and/or facts that, although significant or even crucial, do not necessarily mark the end of a historical phase. For instance, the year 476 CE as the end of the Roman Empire is conventional, since Romulus Augustus was deposed in that year, but the Empire, albeit with remarkable changes, actually survived long past that date. Second, periodization always offers an etic perspective, since in the great majority of the cases, it is the historians' own perception that leads a specific periodization of a time, phase, or era in what D. Blackbourn

---

32 The concept of "infosphere" was introduced by Luciano Floridi and it is defined as "lo spazio semantico costituito dalla totalità dei documenti, degli agenti e delle loro operazioni" [the semantic space constituted by the totality of the documents, of the agents, and of their operations] (Floridi 2002). Of course, the Hittites and their neighbors did not share the totality of the infosphere, but the degree of the circulation of the information was certainly higher than in the previous period, at least on an international level.

33 Bloch 1992.

34 Le Goff 1992.

defines as "conceptual units".[35] Third, it is strictly related not only to the temporal axis but also to the spatial axis: In fact, expressions like "the Italian Renaissance" or "the France of Louis XIV" have been used by historians for decades.[36]

The truth, however, is that it is practically impossible to eliminate periodization: Even the distinction between BCE and CE presupposes a periodization of history, so too does the idea of past and present.[37] Furthermore, the tripartition of Antiquity, the Middle Ages, and Modernity still has some influence. As W. Green wrote in the 1990s, "periodization is rooted in historical theory. It reflects our priorities, our values, and our understanding of the forces, continuity and change"[38]. Indeed, periodization is hard to avoid, despite efforts the of historians like R. Koselleck and F. Braudel, who since the end of World War II addressed the problem of historical time which led, as shown in section 1.2, to the concept of multitemporalities. However, it is not necessary to completely eliminate periodization, since it is sufficient to remember that each periodization represents an etic perspective, and that in ancient cultures it is unusual to find an emic periodization, as is the case for the Hittites, who did not leave any reflections or clues about their own periodization of their history.

Hittite history has not been and still is not immune to etic periodization.

The duration of Hittite history, as meant by the etic periodization of modern historians, is determined by the duration of the written sources from the capital Ḫattuša, meaning that it lasted for about 450 years, from the middle of the 17th to the beginning of the 12th century BCE. These 450 years have been subject to several kinds of periodization, due to different factors such as language, the event-related history, the succession of the kings and what was narrated in the written sources.

The periodization of Hittite history was (and partially still is) influenced by several factors. First, for several decades the sequence of the kings could not be established with certainty and some lines of succession are still debated, in particular the predecessors of Tutḫaliya I.[39]

Second, the language clearly shows three phases, with specific paleographic and linguistic features: Old, Middle, and New Hittite, the last of which further developed into Late New Hittite. However, as A. Archi stated "linguistic periodization

35 Blackbourn 2012, 301.

36 Lorenz 2017, in particular p. 122.

37 See Lorenz 2017.

38 Green 1995, 99.

39 See Götze 1968, Gurney 1974, Freu 1987 and 2002, Klinger 1995, Stavi 2011 and 2015. See also, concerning the sequence of the successors of Telipinu, the list related to the land donations in Rüster / Wilhelm 2012, 58.

and, above all, graphic customs do not necessarily go hand in hand with historical periods"[40], therefore it has been long debated whether a historical phase that can be defined as "Middle Kingdom" could ever be historically identified.

From this perspective it is also important to mention that the majority of the written records have been dated to the Late Hittite period, while documents from the earlier phases are scarce.[41] In particular, the historical narratives dealing with the kings between Telipinu and Tutḫaliya I are almost completely absent, which has led to different evaluation of this period of time, since the very beginning of Hittitology.[42]

The possibly most debated topic was (and still is) the period between Telipinu and Tutḫaliya I, and in more general terms, the beginning of the Hittite Empire.

The first – and in some ways the traditional – threefold periodization was proposed by E. Forrer, who defined these three periods as *altes Ḫatti-Reich*, *mittleres Ḫatti-Reich* and *neues Ḫatti-Reich*, following the terminology of the periodization of Ancient Egypt and preferring the term "New Kingdom" instead of Empire, which would later become common, and indicating Šuppiluliuma I as the king under whose authority the New Kingdom began.[43]

According to A. Götze, the Empire began with Tutḫaliya I, while the period from Telipinu to Tutḫaliya was a gap for which he did not use a specific term at first.[44]

The terminology *mittleres Reich* was used by H. Otten to define the period between the end of the reign of Telipinu and the beginning of the reign of Šuppiluliuma I.[45]

The fact that on a linguistic and paleographic level Middle Hittite can be clearly distinguished from Old and New Hittite sustained the periodization of three periods, and the dating of the Middle Kingdom to the time between Telipinu and Šuppiluliuma became "traditional".[46]

A. Archi in particular questioned the equation of Middle Hittite with the Middle Kingdom period, and in particular the dating of the beginning of the Empire to

---

40 Archi 2003, 5.

41 See, for the dating of the single documents https://www.hethport.uni-wuerzburg.de/hetkonk/hetkonk_abfrageF.php (last access 27/01/2025).

42 I will not take on the problem of Hittite chronology, since it goes far beyond the scope of this research. For reference see, among others, Wilhelm / Boese 1987, Astour 1989, Wilhelm 1991, de Martino 1993 (with previous studies).

43 Forrer 1926.

44 Götze 1928. For the same periodization see also Gurney 1952, Laroche 1955, Bittel 1976, 306, Cornelius 1979, *passim*.

45 Otten 1951.

46 Klengel 1999, 85–134.

the reign of Šuppiluliuma I.[47] This led to a double periodization and to the definition of the period between Tutḫaliya I and Šuppiluliuma I as "Early Empire".[48] However, this twofold view of Hittite history is still a periodization. A different periodization can be found in the volume *The Kingdom of the Hittites* by T. Bryce, in which the author outlines the history of the Hittites according to the sequence of the kings, without further periodization.[49]

The recently published *Handbook Hittite Empire*, edited by S. de Martino,[50] avoids periodization either with or without the Middle Kingdom. However, periodization is still present, since Hittite history is divided into "The Dawn of the Hittite Kingdom", "The Expansion of Hatti and Resistance to Unification", "The Restoration of Order: Telipinu, Pretender or Reformer?", "A Turning Point in the History of Hatti: The Reign of Tuthaliya I", "The Imperial Dimension", "Divine Punishment: The Plague and its Political and Economic Effects", "A New Political Vision and the Transfer of the Capital", "The Reign of Hattušili III: Looking for Legitimacy and Stability".[51] In this handbook the traditional method of periodization is no longer present, and there is an attempt to go over periodization by presenting Hittite history according to historical-political events that constitute – at least from what we can infer from the written sources – pivotal points and/or changes in the political, economic, social, and religious structure of Ḫatti. Nonetheless, this way of presenting Hittite history is also conventional and dependent on an etic perspective, just like any other type of periodization.

It is, of course, impossible to solve the fundamental problem, since the written record gives us no clue about any emic system of periodization. Also, periodization can still have a didactic function.

Since periodization is – by definition – conventional and etic, I think that for the sake of this research a pragmatic approach is needed. First, it is important to be aware of the issues that can influence the way(s) we periodize Hittite history and therefore to be aware that whatever periodization we choose, it will always be shaped – at least partially – by these issues. Second, we have to consider the case studies. Since, as it will be shown in the next paragraph, one case study is the reign of Telipinu and its aftermath, in other words, the transition between Old and Middle Kingdom, and the others – the Battle of Qadesh, the reign of Ḫattušili III, the end of the Hittite Empire – are set in a scenario in which Ḫatti is part

47 Archi 2003.

48 Among others Archi 2005, Gerçek 2017.

49 Bryce 2005.

50 See de Martino (ed.) 2022.

51 de Martino 2022a, 205–270.

of the Great Powers' Club, i. e. from the reign of Šuppiluliuma I onward, the reference to Old Kingdom, Middle Kingdom, and Empire is still the most suitable.

1.4 The Case Studies

The choice of the case studies is determined by various factors. Firstly, the availability and reliability of written sources is an important element for selecting the case studies.

While not all cases have the same number or variety of sources, as well as different textual genres and geographical origins, it is essential to ensure that the case studies are, broadly speaking, well-documented. This allows for a comprehensive understanding of the type of crisis each case represents, as well as the (a)synchronic perception of these crises.

A further factor that must be considered is that all case studies have already been defined as crises by the scholarship, or at the very least, the critical aspect of each case has already been emphasized. This has two consequences. First, it reveals how contemporary historians perceive and evaluate each individual case study, providing a basis for comparison with other perspectives. Second, it allows for a focused analysis of specific elements to understand the nature of the crisis represented by each case study.

Going back to the definitions of R. Koselleck, a crisis can be: 1. "a chain of events leading to a culminating, decisive point at which action is required", 2. "a unique and final point", 3. "a permanent or conditional category pointing to a critical situation which may constantly recur or else to situations in which decisions have momentous consequences", and 4. "a historically immanent transitional phase".[52]

Indeed, the selection of the case studies is based on the criteria discussed above, but it is, in the end, a personal choice. Indeed the correlation between a single case study and a specific definition of crisis can be further discussed, since a single case study may be able to fit two or maybe even more definitions. My goal is to show how the study of specific cases, defined according to precise criteria, point towards a variety of (a)synchronic perceptions of the crises and, consequently, how multitemporality plays an important role in the construction of these perceptions.

Within Hittite history, I have chosen four case studies, each of which fits one of Koselleck's definitions of a crisis.

52 Koselleck 2006, 371–372.

The Battle of Qadesh, fought between the Hittites and Egyptians, serves as a prime example of a crisis in which a series of events culminated in a pivotal moment. In this case, I will highlight the importance of asynchronicity in shaping the perception of the crisis from various perspectives.

The definition of crisis as a final point describes perfectly the crisis that ultimately led to the fall of the Hittite Empire or at the very least, the end of the written records from Ḫattuša and of the regional system as it was structured in the Late Bronze Age. In this particular case, the concept of multiple temporalities can be applied, not only in regard to the historical events that caused the empire's demise, but first and foremost in terms of how this final crisis is perceived.

A perfect example of a crisis that can be considered a historically immanent transitional phase is the reign of Ḫattušili III. Traditionally, the reign of Ḫattušili III is seen as the apogee of the Hittite Empire and not considered a time of crisis. However, I will show how the sources reveal the crucial moments of this king's reign as critical.

Finally, the most complex case study is the reign of Telipinu, which marks, according to the traditional periodization of Hittite history,[53] the transition from the Old Kingdom to the Middle Kingdom. This case study is particularly complex for two reasons. Firstly, the available sources are limited, which has inevitably led to a variety of interpretations of this period. Secondly, the narrative is only the one of Telipinu without the possibility of confronting it with other sources. However, I believe it is possible to demonstrate that this period can be described as a crisis perceived as a critical situation that could recur.

On a methodological level, each case study will be presented individually. First the main features of each case will be presented, and then the available sources will be surveyed, in order to understand which different perspectives are represented, and how and why the sources have been interpreted.

The second step of the investigation is a survey of the sources and a discussion of the secondary literature on the case study. In particular, where they are available, the different interpretations will be outlined.

The third and crucial step is the comparison of the data from the sources with their modern interpretations in order to discover and describe the perception of each crisis from the three different perspectives and to show how (a)synchronicity works in each case.

The goals are various: first, to find out whether a crisis is perceived as such by all three perspectives, why it is or isn't and how is this supported by the sources; second, to underline (a)synchronicity, to understand where it comes from and

53 See Ch. 2.1.

how it works; third, to reflect on the consequences of (a)synchronicity and multitemporality in the evaluation of crises in ancient history.

2 The Case Studies

2.1 Case Study #1 The Proclamation of Telipinu: Misleading Perceptions

2.1.1 Why the Proclamation of Telipinu?

The first case study is probably both the most complex and, at the same time, the easiest, for one and the same reason: the leading written sources consist of only one document, the so-called "Proclamation" or "Edict" of Telipinu (CTH 19).[54]

This does not mean that this text is the only source dating to the reign of Telipinu[55] but it is the only one that contains a narrative with aspects that can be interpreted as critical and therefore it perfectly fits the purpose of this study. Furthermore, in comparison to the other case studies, it is possible to make significant remarks on asynchronicity and how it works by considering only a single document.

The Proclamation of Telipinu represents a very suitable case study for crises in Hittite history. On the one hand, the reign of Telipinu is considered, when the standard periodization of Old and Middle Kingdom is employed, the end of the Old Kingdom and the period of passage to the Middle Kingdom. Furthermore, in comparison with the documentation of the Empire, the sources of the Old and Middle Kingdom are scarce and the Proclamation of Telipinu can therefore shed some light on the previous periods (with the caveat that it represents the political agenda of Telipinu and not an objective report of the facts). More precisely, the Proclamation makes manifest (more or less willingly) that the succession to the throne represents a critical moment not only at the time of Telipinu but also, recurringly, almost from the beginning of the Hittite history. In other words, the Proclamation of Telipinu shows that the moment of the succession to the throne may represent a crisis, more specifically a recurring one. Since, as it will be shown more in depth in the next paragraph, the Proclamation also contains a norm concerning the regulation of the succession to the throne, it is possible to interpret this norm as the decision with potentially momentous consequences that represents a solution to the crisis.

54 See below, Ch. 2.1.2. The definition of the genre goes beyond the purpose of this study. However, for a relatively recent study, see Mora 2008, specifically 305–307.

55 See also CTH 20 and 21 as well as some of the land donations (on these texts see Rüster / Wilhelm 2012, in particular 38–39).

 https://doi.org/10.1515/9783111712383-004

Before analyzing this case study and to present the Proclamation in more depth, it is necessary to more fully define the kind of crisis that it represents.

It must be mentioned that the Proclamation of Telipinu has received particular attention from the scholarship, since it has been considered a "reform" of the succession to the Hittite throne and because the text contains a long section underlining the struggles during the succession to the throne as a recurring event, also involving the succession to the throne of Telipinu himself (CTH 19, obv. i 1 – ii 35).

The lengthy "historical" or "narrative" section of the Proclamation and then the issue of the regulation of the succession to the throne may reflect a crisis that can be defined as "a permanent or conditional category pointing to a critical situation which may constantly recur or else to situations in which decisions have momentous consequences".[56]

The questions that need to be asked in order to evaluate whether the Proclamation of Telipinu describes a specific type of crisis are: 1. What are the elements that point to this definition of crisis, and why? 2. Is such a crisis perceived synchronically by the three perspectives considered, i.e. the Hittite perspective, that of the neighboring polities, and ours as historians?

In order to answer these questions, it is necessary to delve into the content of the Proclamation.

2.1.2 The Text

The so-called "Edict" or "Proclamation" of Telipinu (CTH 19) represents, for several reasons, a particularly puzzling document among the Hittite written sources.

Traditionally, scholars have viewed the text as consisting of two distinct parts: one "historical" or "narrative" section that recounts the events leading to Telipinu's decision to issue a regulation on succession to the throne, and another containing various regulations on different topics.[57]

The first part, encompassing paragraphs 1–28, includes the "narrative" and the regulation on the succession to the throne. The second, paragraphs 29–50, covers a range of topics, including the relationships within the royal family, as well as sealings of goods, murder, and sorcery. The majority of studies on the Edict of Telipinu have focused on the first part of the document. It has been viewed as a valuable source, sometimes the only one available, for reconstructing early Hittite his-

56 See fn. 6.

57 Edition: Hoffmann 1984. For all the studies on the text, see https://www.hethport.uni-wuerzburg.de/hetkonk/hetkonk_abfrage.php?c=19 (last access 30/09/2024).

tory[58] Additionally, it has been interpreted as a form of propaganda or a manifesto of Hittite royal ideology.[59] Scholars have also examined the genre of the document, labeling it an "edict",[60] a "proclamation"[61], or more specifically a "constitution".[62]

The first part, the narrative section, presents a specific structure that has been described by the scholarship as three-fold in a scheme that can be summarized as good → bad → good. These three parts and the consequent labels of "good" or "bad" coincide with specific periods of time starting with the reign of Labarna and ending with the reign of Telipinu.

More precisely, the first good period is relatively short and lasts only for the reign of Labarna, Ḫattušili I and Muršili I (obv. i 2–34); then the bad period, characterized by murders within the royal family and struggles for the throne, lasts from Ḫantili I to Ḫuzziya I (obv. i 35 – ii 15), the last predecessor of Telipinu with whom the new "good" period starts.

The passage of the texts that is likely most debated concerns the regulation of the succession to the throne and states:

> King shall become a son (who is a) prince of first rank only. If there is no first rank prince, he who is a son of second rank shall become king. If there is no prince, (no) male, she who is a first rank princess, for her they shall take an in-marrying (son-in-law) and he shall become king (CTH 19, obv. ii 36–39).[63]

Furthermore, from this passage some consequences arise that flow into a ruling concerning bloodshed within the royal family:

> Who will become king after me in future, let his brothers, his sons, his in-laws, his (further) family members and his troops be united! You will come (and) hold the country subdued with (your) might. And do not speak as follows: 'I will clean (it) out', for you will not clean anything. On the contrary, you will get involved yourself. Do not kill anybody of your family. It (is) not right. Furthermore, whoever becomes king and seeks evil for (his) brother (or) sister, you too are his Council and tell him straight: 'This (is) a matter of blood'. Look at the tablet (that says): 'Formerly, blood(shed) became excessive in Hattusa, and the gods took it out on the royal family'. If anyone does evil amongst both (his) brothers and sisters and lays eyes

58 This was, however, a tendency of the earliest scholarship. On the misuse of the Proclamation for historical reconstruction see Liverani 1977.

59 See Gilan 2015, 137–177 with previous literature.

60 Hoffmann's edition labels the text *Erlaß* (Hoffmann 1984).

61 Among others, van den Hout 2003 and Goedegebuure 2006b.

62 *Verfassung:* Haase 2005.

63 Translation after van den Hout 2003, 196.

> on the king's head, summon the assembly and, if h[i]s testimony is dismissed, he shall pay with his head. They shall not kill secretly (CTH 19, obv. ii 40–52).[64]

These passages have been traditionally considered the core of the Proclamation, since they contain what has been interpreted as the "reform" of the rule concerning the succession to the throne. Furthermore, the long narrative section before this rule has been interpreted as functional to it.

Needless to say, the historical narrative cannot be considered an accurate and objective report of the facts,[65] as already pointed out in the early studies of M. Liverani[66] and H. Hoffner,[67] since Telipinu followed his own political agenda by issuing the Proclamation. In particular, it is possible to recognize, as the previous scholarship already did, two goals that Telipinu wanted to achieve with his Proclamation: 1. The justification of his own dubious ascension to the throne, since he was not the heir presumptive and was not supposed to become king; 2. The regulation of the succession to the throne and a specific ruling related to murders and consequent punishment within the royal family. Even though these two goals have found consensus among scholars, I want to point out a critical statement by M. Liverani that shed a different light on the interpretation of this narrative and that is functional to the interpretation of the crisis that the Proclamation represents. Liverani states, in fact, that Telipinu: "non contrappone così una nuova legge migliore ad una vecchia legge inadeguata; contrappone l'inizio dell'applicazione della legge al precedente periodo di illegalità".[68]

This position of M. Liverani suggests that this passage of the Proclamation, and therefore the text in its entirety, does not represent a "reform", meaning it does not issue a new rule for the succession to the throne that substitutes for a different, previous rule, but instead puts in written form a norm that was probably already in use. The innovation is the written form, which constitutes also the strength of the norm, and its enforcement.

Since the last part of the text deals with further administrative rules (rev. iii 4 – iv 34), it is possible that the regulation of the succession to the throne was also interpreted as a reform following the same interpretation of the other norms. However, in the case of these norms in the last portion of the text, it is also unknown whether they were indeed innovations of preexisting norms, or whether they were simply current norms put in written form.

---

64 Translation after van den Hout 2003, 196.

65 See also case study #3 in Ch. 2.3.

66 Liverani 1977.

67 Hoffner 1975 and 1980.

68 Liverani 1977, 119.

2.1.3 A Recurring Crisis

Regardless of whether the statement of these norms should be interpreted as a reform or not, which is an interesting topic but not crucial for the evaluation of the crisis, the question of whether the Proclamation of Telipinu is a description of a crisis that could be defined as "a permanent or conditional category pointing to a critical situation which may constantly recur or else to situations in which decisions have momentous consequences" still needs to be answered. Also still open is the consequent question concerning the perception of this crisis by the different actors.

In order to answer these questions, we have to shift our focus. It is indeed relevant to keep in mind the goals of the Proclamation and also how the text has been thus far interpreted, however we must focus more deeply on the general content of the narrative section and of the ruling concerning the succession to the throne and the bloodshed within the royal family.

This is, in fact, exactly the crucial point. Indeed, the narrative in the first part of the Proclamation is adamant that the succession to the throne often constituted a critical moment in Hittite history. Regardless of the accuracy of the details in Telipinu's report, it is indeed possible with a great degree of certainty to confirm that the succession to the throne was a challenging moment throughout Hittite history.[69] In support of this statement, in fact, other written sources, both earlier and later than the Proclamation of Telipinu, depict a very similar picture. Two of the most significant are the so-called "Testament" of Ḫattušili I and the "Apology" of Ḫattušili III.

The so-called "testament" (CTH 6)[70] describes the disinheritance of the heir presumptive (obv. i 1–13):

> [Gr]eat Ki[ng] Tabarna said to the entire army and the dignitaries: I have become ill, (so) I introduced young Labarna to you: "He shall be enthroned." I, the king, called him my son, I continually instructed him, I looked after him constantly. He however showed himself a youth unfit to be seen, he did not cry, he was not kind. Cold he is! He is not kind of heart! I, the king, apprehended him and had him brought to my couch: "Why? Should no one ever again raise his sister's son? (But) he did not accept the advice of the king. The advice of his mother, (that) snake, that he accepted! His brothers and sisters sent cold(-hearted) messages to him, and he always listened to their words. However, I, the king heard (of it), and I entered into a lawsuit";[71] and then the choice of another successor: "Muršili is hereby my son. [Recognize] him instead. It is him you have to enthrone. [. . .]. [The go]d [installs] a(nother)

69 See Beckman 1995.

70 https://www.hethport.uni-wuerzburg.de/hetkonk/hetkonk_abfrage.php?c=6 (last access 30/09/2024).

71 Obv. i 1–13. Translation after Goedegebuure 2006a, 224.

> li[on] in place of the lion. [If at some ti]me the call to arms go[es forth] o[r when] perhaps [a rebellion becom]es [serious], you, my servants and nobles must be [of assistance to my son]".[72] Furthermore, the king also tried to prevent further problem with the succession to the throne: "[Let no o]ne say: 'The king [will] secretly [do] (what is in) his heart. I will consider it right, whether it is true or not.' May defamation never, ever sit right [with you]. You [who yourselves] now acknowledge my words and my wisdom in mind, instruct my son in wisdom![73]

The "Apology" of Ḫattušili III is, if possible, even more explicit in picturing the conflict that occurred within the royal family after the death of Muwatalli II and the succession of Urḫi-Teššup, as will be shown in the third case study.[74]

The Proclamation of Telipinu is therefore the epitome of the way this type of crisis was handled. Not only does it explicitly show that the inheritance of the throne after a king's death was a recurring critical moment in Hittite history, but it also provides a possible blueprint for avoiding such crises in the future, which is a clear sign that the succession to the throne was indeed perceived as a critical moment.

The Proclamation of Telipinu is therefore connected to the crisis on two levels: 1. The long historical narrative clearly describes a "critical situation which may constantly recur"; 2. By putting the norm of the succession in written form, the Proclamation of Telipinu represented an act that has "momentous consequences".

As the Apology of Ḫattušili III clearly shows, the consequences of the decision of Telipinu to put the norm in written form are not as momentous as was expected, since the succession to the throne did not cease to be a critical moment after Telipinu, but the effectivity of the rule was known only to the posterity of Telipinu.

2.1.4 Misleading Perception

Now that we have established that the Proclamation of Telipinu represents that transition of power after the death of a king was a recurring moment of crisis throughout Hittite history (until the reign of Telipinu) and that the decision to clarify the rules of succession in writing had (potentially) momentous consequences, we must acknowledge that the way this type of crisis was perceived by the three different perspectives, i. e. the Hittites, the neighboring polities and us, as his-

72 Obv. i 37–41. Translation after Goedegebuure 2006a, 225.
73 Obv. ii 53–57. Translation after Goedegebuure 2006a, 225.
74 For this specific case, see case study #3 in Ch. 2.3.

torians is still an open question. In other words, were these perspectives in sync or not?

Regarding the perspective of the Hittites, it is fundamental to keep in mind a key point, i.e. to what degree the Hittites were aware of their earlier history. This question does not have a straightforward answer. On the one hand, the fact that early documents were copied and recopied until the end of the Hittite history suggests that the Hittites had a fairly conscious knowledge of their early history. On the other hand, these documents were issued by specific kings and therefore represent their individual political agendas. This means that the way the Hittites perceived their early history was at least partially influenced by the narrative present in these documents.[75]

However, the fact that in the Proclamation of Telipinu (and, as we will see in case study #3, also in the "Apology" of Ḫattušili III) the succession to the throne represented a central topic and that some measures were taken to avoid problems in the future, reveals that the Hittite perceived the recurring succession crisis as synchronic. In fact, they perceived it as an actual crisis that needed to be dealt with.

The perception of this recurring crisis held by neighboring polities is complex to reconstruct since there are no relevant written sources, at least not regarding Hittite history before the reign of Telipinu. Some considerations are however possible. The first is that in the Proclamation the narrative often connects the succession crisis to a broader crisis that led to the loss of territory to foreign enemies, as for instance in the passage in obv. ii, 1–4:

> Now, the land became his enemy: the cities of ...agga, [Matjila, Galmiya, Adaniya], Arzawiya, Šallapa, Parduwata and Aḫḫula. But wherever (his) troops went on campaign, they did not come back successfully.[76]

This might be very well a literary *topos* that served the political agenda of Telipinu, who wanted to present himself as a powerful king on an international level, as well as a domestic one. However, it is not completely far-fetched to think that other polities, knowing about a succession/dynastic crisis, might have tried to take advantage of it. However, the sources just do not provide enough evidence for us to ascertain to what degree the neighboring polities were aware of the fact that the succession to the throne was, among the Hittites, a critical moment,

75 For a closer look at the audience of the texts that contain "historical" narratives see case study #3 in Ch. 2.3.

76 Translation after Goedegebuure 2006b, 231.

and therefore it is not possible to know how much their perspective was in sync with the crisis.

Finally, we as historians perceive the crisis synchronically with what the Proclamation tells in its narrative, since we also have proof, from other sources, that the succession to the throne represented, throughout Hittite history, a potential critical moment.

However, the Proclamation of Telipinu might have misled the perception of the crisis by the Hittites. In fact, the tripartite division of good → bad → good is not consistent with the actual historical events, as is proven by the fact that the succession between Ḫattušili I and Muršili I was also critical, as is shown by the "Testament".

The narrative of the Proclamation is also misleading for us, as historians. For many of the succession crises reported in the Proclamation of Telipinu, there are no other sources with information that helps to prove or disprove the narrative of Telipinu. Therefore, we might perceive the recurrence of the succession crisis as more common than it actually was, especially because the sources support this view for several other cases, for instance the succession of Muršili I, of Šuppiluliuma I, of Muršili IIII, and of Ḫattušili III.

In summary, the Proclamation of Telipinu and its narrative convey a synchronic perception of the crisis from, potentially, all three perspectives, albeit with the necessary caveats considered. At the same time, the fact that the Proclamation is the leading source concerning the recurring crisis of succession may result in misleading generalizations about the type of crisis that succession represented at different points in Hittite history.

2.2 Case Study #2 The Battle of Qadesh: Asynchronicity at Work

2.2.1 Preliminary Remarks

The Battle of Qadesh is a very well-known event in Hittite history, even for a general audience, and therefore does not require a lengthy introductory summary.

However, while I will not describe the battle itself,[77] I will highlight the elements that make the Battle of Qadesh suitable as case study in this work.

77 On this topic see recently Guidotti / Pecchioli Daddi 2002 (eds.) with detailed studies on the military, the strategy, and the phases of the battle, as well as on the protagonists.

As is well known, the Battle of Qadesh can be defined as the showdown between Egypt and Ḫatti after a period of escalating enmity. However, this picture is not as straightforward as it has been, and indeed still is, perceived. Indeed, to reconstruct the reasons that led to the Battle of Qadesh is no easy task and, given the situation of the sources, it is also an easily biased one. As M. Liverani pointed out, the Battle of Qadesh has entered the collective imagination for its "ideological" meaning, as a clash between two "visions of the world"[78], that of the Egyptians and that of the Hittites, as well as for the massive celebratory program of Ramesses II in the aftermath of the battle.[79]

Setting aside the collective imagination, specifically the ideological meaning and the celebratory program of Ramesses II, which play an important role in the perception of the event by the historians, the battle also had geopolitical consequences. In fact, the ambiguous result of the clash not only stopped the Egyptian advance in Syria, but also made the "regional system"[80] stable for the subsequent two centuries. Furthermore, a peace treaty was signed some fifteen years after the battle.[81] What is of particular importance for the purpose of this study is that these consequences are necessarily interpreted with the particular biases inherent in the perceptions of not only the historians, but also of the actors involved in the event, and it is therefore in the evaluation of the battle's meaning (as well as its origins and aftermath) that (a)synchronicity may surface.

Having outlined the crucial elements of the perception of the Battle of Qadesh, two questions are now relevant: 1. How does the Battle of Qadesh represent the "culminating point" of a crisis, as defined in the presentation of the case studies? and 2. What are the elements of (a)synchonicity that may emerge from this event?

To answer the first question, it is first of all crucial to survey the sources regarding not only the Battle of Qadesh as an event *per se*, but also the sources that may contain clues regarding the events leading up to the clash, as well as the ones concerning the aftermath, and to assess them all, so that we can understand whether or not the Battle of Qadesh was the peak of a crisis between Ḫatti and Egypt that had already begun (long) before the actual conflict occurred, and how relations later developed between the two polities after the battle.

As previously mentioned, the sources are far from complete and unbiased, therefore a comparison between them is crucial in order to answer the second question. In particular, it is necessary to point out not only the perception of the

78 Liverani 2002. See also Liverani 1994 and Archi 2002.

79 Specifically, on the Ramesside propaganda and the Hittites see Liverani 1990.

80 See fn. 17.

81 Edition: Edel 1997.

Battle of Qadesh as single event but also of it as culminating point of a crisis. Finally, it is also relevant to question the sources about the crisis itself, to consider how they contain elements that point to it, and especially how these elements were perceived by the different actors involved. On this note, it needs to be stated that battles such as the one in Qadesh were rare in the preclassic period, however, smaller conflicts were endemic.[82] Therefore, the question of whether the Battle of Qadesh was perceived as a peak moment of the crisis is a general one, because it deals with the question of how this kind of clash was perceived by the actors involved. In particular, even if it is clear that these events are considered to be diriment points in history, their perception might have been asynchronic for some or all of the protagonists.

2.2.2 The Sources

The sources related to the Battle of Qadesh represent the first consistent occurrence of asynchronicity. The Egyptian sources are contemporary to the reign of Ramesses II, while the Hittite sources are all dated to the period after the death of Muwatalli II, the Hittite king who fought at Qadesh. The sources also present a notable disparity between the Egyptian and Hittite narratives of the event. Contemporary Egyptian sources from the reign of Ramesses II provide a consistent narrative, while Hittite sources convey only scattered and scarce information. This discrepancy can be attributed to several factors. First, Ramesses II objectively had a much longer reign than Muwatalli II – who died shortly after the Battle of Qadesh – which allowed for a longer date range for Egyptian sources concerning the battle and dated to the time of Ramesses II, since the protagonist of the battle was still alive. While the exact duration of Muwatalli II's reign is uncertain,[83] it is worth noting that Ramesses II's reign encompassed also the reigns of Muwatalli's first two successors Urḫi-Teššup (Muršili III), Ḫattušili III, and, partially, the reign of Tutḫaliya IV. Second, there are very few recovered Hittite texts that can be attributed to Muwatalli II. This may be due to happenstance, since we only have access to the texts we have found, and it must be remembered there may have been more texts produced that simply did not survive or have not yet been found, and it is possible that Muwatalli's decision to move the capital of the Hittite kingdom

82 Liverani 2002.

83 For an overview of the reign of this king see Bryce 2005, 221–245 and, more specifically and more recently, Doğan-Alparslan 2012.

from Ḫattuša in the North to Tarḫuntašša in the South[84] played a role in the scarcity of texts from his reign among the written sources from Ḫattuša. Because the exact location of Tarḫuntašša in southeastern Anatolia remains unknown,[85] it is speculative but not far-fetched to imagine the possibility that the majority of the written sources from Muwatalli's reign may still be lying unearthed in the new capital.

However, this does not mean that there are no Hittite sources about the Battle of Qadesh. It simply means that there is no source from the exact time period of the battle or written by the Hittite king who participated in the battle.

The sources from Ḫatti are, however, few and none of them explicitly mention the Battle of Qadesh.

The first text is CTH 81, the so-called "Apology" of Ḫattušili III. In obv. ii 69–73 we read:

> Now, when it happened, that my brother went to Egypt, I led for my brother on campaign down to Egypt the troops (and) chariots of those lands which I had resettled, and I commanded the troops (and) chariots of Hatti-Land of which I was in charge in front of my brother.[86]

It is clear that here the focus is not the clash itself but the fact that Ḫattušili participated in it with his own troops, since the goal is to underline his power.

A similar tone is taken in a passage of the decree of Ḫattušili concerning the estate of Arma-Tarḫunta KUB 21.17, obv. i 14–21:

> Since Muwatalli, my brother, fought against the king of Egypt and the king of Amurru, when he defeated the king of Egypt and the king of Amurru, he then went to Aba. When my brother Muwatalli defeated Aba, he came back to Ḫatti, but I was there, in Aba.[87]

In this case the personal political agenda of Ḫattušili is still present, although presented more subtly and the passage seems to report the facts in a more neutral fashion.

The facts are also reported in the third and last document from Ḫattuša, a letter from Ramesses to Ḫattušili, KBo 1.15++, obv. 15–40 in which the battle is described in more detail:

---

84 The reasons for the move of the capital are not certain, yet the hypothesis of Singer 2006 of a failed religious reform remains seminal.

85 See Alp 1995, Yakar *et al.* 2000, Dinçol *et al.* 2000 and 2001, Bahar / Çay / İscan 2007, Melchert 2007, Forlanini 2017.

86 Translation van den Hout 2003, 201–202.

87 Edition: Ünal 1974, 18–31, transliteration and (German) translation of the passage p. 20–21.

> Furthermore, concerning the enmity of Ḫatti with Egypt, you wrote to me as follows: 'Do not you think anymore to the days of the enemies of Ḫatti?' This you wrote to me. That was the enmity of a god and caused me troubles but I went amidst the enemies of Ḫatti and killed these enemies, when the army of Muwatalli, king of Ḫatti, came with the many countries that were with him, while the armies of the great king, the king of Egypt, were still in the land of Amurru, in the land of ... and in the land of Taminta. And when the vanguard of the great king, the king of Egypt, reached the city of Shabtuna, two Bedouins from the army of the country of Ḫatti came to the king and said thus: 'The king of Ḫatti is in the country of Aleppo.' Three armies are approaching on the roads, and they had not yet reached the place where the king was. The king was sitting on his throne on the western bank of the Orontes River and the vanguard was in the field that they were planting and occupying. And while the king knew that Muwatalli, the king of Ḫatti, had left the country of Aleppo, the king did not know his intentions. And the king of Ḫatti attacked him by surprise with his army and with all the countries that were with him but the king of Egypt caused his defeat completely by himself although my troops were not with me and although my chariot fighters were not with me. And I led away the enemies of these countries of the country of Ḫatti into the country of Egypt before the sons of the land of Egypt and before the sons of the land of Ḫatti. And then you could say about my army: 'The army was not there, and the charioteers were not there?' You see, one army of mine was inside the land of Amurru, another army of mine in the land of ... and another army in the land of Taminta, and these are the facts.[88]

This is an interesting letter because it is the only explicit exchange of information concerning the battle between Ḫatti and Egypt, however, it is not a Hittite source, though it was found at Ḫattusa, instead the letter was sent by Ramesses and, unfortunately, the reply of Hattusili is unknown. If, on the one hand, in this letter Ramesses narrates the phases of the battle according to his propagandistic agenda, on the other hand, it is interesting that the letter underlines that "these are the facts", as it may represent an attempt to establish, for both actors involved, an official version of the events, and therefore an official narrative.

The Egyptian sources are not greater in number, but they are from the time of Ramesses II and specifically report the battle.

The Egyptian sources are divided by the scholarship into "poems" and "bulletins", with the former being texts of literary nature, the latter being the narratives that accompany the reliefs.

The bulletins are present in some of the most important temples and monuments, like Abydos, Karnak, Luxor, the Ramesseum, and Abu Simbel. The poems are present in the Papyrus Raifé / Sallier III, and in the Papyrus Chester Beatty III.[89]

88 Edition: Edel 1994, 58–65.

89 For a complete list and a synopsis see Breyer 2010, 214–215.

Both the bulletin and the poem are very long and elaborate texts that report the events of the Battle of Qadesh in great detail, focusing especially on three points: 1. The role of Ramesses in the battle, in particular underlining his decisions; 2. The treachery of the Hittites and their allies; 3. The Egyptian victory.[90]

Since the Battle of Qadesh may be defined as the "culminating point" of a crisis, it crucial to understand how the relations between Ḫatti and Egypt were both before and after the Battle of Qadesh. We already saw that after the Battle of Qadesh relations slowly took a turn toward an alliance between the two polities, and it is also easy to follow the development of the relations after the Battle of Qadesh thanks to the more than one hundred letters exchanged between Ramesses and Ḫattušili and their families and dignitaries.[91]

However, it is also possible to follow – at least to some extent – the unfolding of relations between Ḫatti and Egypt before the Battle of Qadesh, since some Hittite texts shed light to the period leading to the clash.

In particular, I want to focus my attention on three documents that will be discussed in the next paragraph: 1. The Kuruštama treaty (CTH 134), probably concluded just before Šuppiluliuma's reign or even during his reign;[92] 2. The Deeds of Šuppiluliuma (CTH 40), which narrates the famous *daḫamunzu*-episode[93]; 3. The Second Plague Prayer (CTH 378.2) of Muršili with references to the events reported in CTH 40, but with a different narrative.[94]

The Kuruštama treaty is very fragmentary, however it clearly describes the alliance and good relations between Egypt and Ḫatti:

> The men of Ḫ[atti], you should not go into the land of E[gypt] with [ev]il intentions, [and the men of Egypt should not go into] the land of Ḫatti [with?] evil. [The land of Ḫ]attuša [should] be allies to the land of Egypt and you should defend Egypt! Egypt should be allies [to Ḫattuša and should defend Ḫattuša].[95]

90 For a complete translation of the texts, see Kitchen 1996, 2–26.
91 See Edel 1994.
92 See Devecchi 2015, 265. For the edition of the text see Singer 2004.
93 For the entire report of the crisis with Egypt see Del Monte 2009, 112–129. For an English translation of the deeds see Güterbock 1956. For further studies see https://www.hethport.uni-wuerzburg.de/hetkonk/hetkonk_abfrage.php?c=40 (last access 27/01/2025).
94 For an overview of the history of research, of the manuscripts, a transliteration, and a translation see E. Rieken *et al.* (eds.), hethiter.net/: CTH 378.2 (INTR 2016–01–18). For an English translation see Singer 2002, 57–61 and van den Hout 2006, 263–266. There is possibly a reference to the treaty in the fragmentary prayer CTH 379, obv. ii 6–24, as suggested by Singer 2004.
95 CTH 134, rev. 5–10, after the reconstruction of Singer 2004, 601–602.

The Deeds of Šuppiliuma offers the most complete explanation of the *casus belli* that instigated the hostility between Ḫatti and Egypt, at least according to the Hittite sources, and more specifically according to the narrative of Muršili II.

The text is relatively rich in details and it can be summarized as follows:[96]

- Šuppiluliuma receives a letter from the widow of the Egyptian Pharaoh Nibḫururiya[97] who ask for a son of the Hittite king to marry.[98]
- The Hittite king is perplexed by the message, as he states: “Such a thing has never happened to me in my whole life!”,[99] and suspecting that the Egyptian are setting a trap, sends Ḫattušaziti to Egypt with the purpose of knowing more about the odd request of the queen.[100]
- When Ḫattušaziti return from Egypt with the confirmation that the letter was indeed true, as well as the request of the queen[101], Šuppiluliuma, after having verified that there was an agreement between Ḫatti and Egypt, states: “Of old, Ḫattuša and Egypt were friendly with each other, and now this, too, on our behalf, has taken place between t[hem]! Thus: Ḫatti and Egypt will continuously be friendly with each other!” and decides to send his son Zannanza to be the new husband of the Egyptian widow.[102]
- However, Zannanza is killed before arriving in Egypt and the good relations between the two countries are destroyed.[103]

Finally, in the Second Plague Prayer, the beginning of the hostility between Ḫatti and Egypt is also reported, however in different terms than in the Deeds. In the text we read:

> The second tablet concerned the town of Kuruštamma – how the Stormgod of Ḫatti brought the men of Kuruštamma to the land of Egypt; and how the Stormgod of Ḫatti made a treaty between them and the men of Ḫatti, so that they were put under oath by the Stormgod of Ḫatti. Since the of Ḫatti and the men of Egypt were bound under oath by the Stormgod of Ḫatti, and the men of Ḫatti proceeded to get the upper hand, the men of Ḫatti thereby broke the oath of the gods at once. My father sent infantry and chariotry, and they attacked the border territory of Egypt, the land of Amka. And again he sent, and again they attacked. When the men of Egypt became afraid. They came, and they asked my father outright for his

96 An English translation of the narrative is offered by Güterbock 1956, 94–97.
97 The identity of Nibḫururiya is not clear yet, see Miller 2007.
98 KBo 5.6, rev. iii 1–19.
99 KBo 5.6, rev. iii 18–19.
100 KBo 5.6, rev. iii 20–25.
101 KBo 5.6, rev. iii 44 – iv 15.
102 KBo 14.12++, rev. iv 1–40.
103 KUB 19.4++, obv. 3–23. The actual circumstances of the death of Zannanza are still debated, since the text is fragmentary.

> son for kingship. But when my father gave them his son, they led him off, they killed him. And my father became angry, and he went into Egyptian territory, and he attacked the Egyptians and he destroy the Egyptian infantry and chariotry.[104]

It is clear, as has already been pointed out by the scholarship, that the different narratives depend on the different purposes of the documents.[105]

A further group of texts must be mentioned as explicative of the Hittite-Egyptian relations before the Battle of Qadesh: the letters of El-Amarna.[106] Only four of the El-Amarna letters (EA 41, EA 42, EA 43, EA 44) were exchanged with the Hittite king (Šuppiluliuma I) and his court (specifically a son of the Hittite king) and they clearly describe positive relations between Ḫatti and Egypt, as shown by the family metaphors used by the actors to refer to each other, in particular the term "brother" used by the two kings, as well as by the exchange of gifts mentioned in EA 41 (lines 39–43) and 44 (lines 25–29, although some statements demonstration bumpier relations concerning specific topics, e.g. ranking, as the question of the Hittite king:

> Why did you put your name over my name? (EA 42, line 15)

makes clear. However, this does not seem to indicate the breaking of the alliance or a state of hostility between the two polities, since the fact that letters were exchanged is evidence that the diplomatic dialogue was still ongoing.

Before discussing relations between Egypt and Ḫatti and the events that led to the Battle of Qadesh, it is necessary to point out some important aspects of the sources considered.

Since this study considers the perspective of the Hittites and the neighboring polities, i.e., in this case study, of the actors more or less actively involved in the Battle of Qadesh, the visibility or accessibility of the sources is crucial. Even if our understanding of what kind of audience had access to the sources in general (and mostly to the written texts, given the low rate of literacy)[107] is to a certain degree speculative, the monumental dimension of some of the Egyptian sources show that the goal of these sources was to be both visible and accessible, even though only to a selected audience. On the other hand, the scarce Hittite sources are only brief

---

104 CTH 378.2, obv. 13–24. For the translation of the passage see Singer 2002, 58.

105 A summary of Muršili's propaganda on this topic can be found in Pallavidini 2016a, 257–261 with further references.

106 For an English translation of the letters see Moran 1992. For a detailed study see Mynářová 2007.

107 Michalowski 2015.

references to the battle or more elaborate narratives on the period preceding the clash written on clay tablets, and therefore not necessarily visible. Regarding the contemporary accessibility of the Hittite sources, it is relevant to note that the texts belong to different genres that probably had different levels of diffusion among the audience, who was, however, even more limited than the one of the Egyptian sources.[108] There is a third element that has to be considered: the goals of the sources. Considering the differences in the visibility and accessibility, one might think that the goal of the Hittite sources was less influenced by reasons of propaganda than the one of the Egyptian sources. Nonetheless both sides aimed either to build a specific narrative of the Battle of Qadesh (the Egyptian side) or of the events before and after it (the Hittite side), therefore both are – to some extent – propagandistic. The audiences and the purpose of the propaganda might be (partially) different, but none of the source represents a reliable report of the battle or of the events leading up to it.

2.2.3 The Unfolding of the Hittite-Egyptian Relations

The history of relations between Ḫatti and Egypt is a thoroughly studied topic, probably because of the relevance in the collective imagination of the Battle of Qadesh and of the peace treaty signed in the aftermath.

The literature on the topic is therefore immense, and it is beyond the purpose of this work to discuss it at length. However, it is important to set some firm points. The interest in the topic started at the beginning of the 1900s with a study by B. Meissner that considered the Hittite sources concerning the relations between Ḫatti and Egypt,[109] one by K. Sethe concerning the Egyptian sources[110] and one other by E. Cavaignac with the title "L'Égypte et le Hatti vers 1302".[111]

The interest in the relations between Ḫatti and Egypt continued throughout the following decades[112] with a pivotal study by W. Murnane dedicated specifically to the Battle of Qadesh.[113] Some twenty years later another study dedicated to the

108 See, specifically on the audience of the "deeds", Gilan 2005.
109 Meissner 1918.
110 Sethe 1926.
111 Cavaignac 1935–1937.
112 See e.g. Carruba 1976, Del Monte 1985, Archi 1997, De Vos 2007. These contributions are dedicated to the Hittite-Egyptian relations in general, of course there is a huge number of studies dedicated to specific aspects or events regarding these relations. On the significant topic of the Hittite-Egyptian synchronisms see recently Devecchi / Miller 2011 with previous literature.
113 Murnane 1990.

Battle of Qadesh with contribution by Hittitologists as well as Egyptologists appeared as a collective volume edited by F. Pecchioli Daddi and M.C. Guidotti.[114] Some years ago a monumental monograph dedicated to the relations between Ḫatti and Egypt was published by F. Breyer, and it can be still considered the most updated and all-encompassing work on the topic.[115]

From the sources available and also from the secondary literature, it is possible to define several different phases in the development of the Hittite-Egyptian relations:

- Phase 0 = Before Šuppiluliuma I. Even though the only source available is the Kuruštama treaty (CTH 134) and the references to it in the Deeds of Šuppiluliuma (CTH 40), it is of great importance in delineating this phase of the relations between Ḫatti and Egypt. As a matter of fact the presence of a treaty or at least of some agreement between the two countries is a sign of reciprocal good relations.
- Phase 1 = The reign of Šuppiluliuma I. As already pointed out, this phase is very rich in sources. However, only the letters from El-Amarna are coeval with the reign of this Hittite king, while the others are not synchronic with Šuppiluliuma's reign, since they date to the reign of his son Muršili II. Even if the goal of Muršili II is to highlight the reasons of his enmity with Egypt, nonetheless these sources trace in a relatively detailed manner the development, and especially the worsening, of the relations between the two countries. The well known episode of the *daḫamunzu*, in fact, can described as the peak of the good relations, since Egypt and Ḫatti were close to a solid alliance through a marriage[116] and this ascendent parabola is testified to by the direct reference to the Kuruštama-treaty and by the report of Ḫattusaziti about the good intentions of the Egyptian queen. However, the death of Zannanza made the curve descend quickly and unexpectedly, and marks the end of good relations between Ḫatti and Egypt.
- Phase 3 = The period between the death of Zannanza and the Battle of Qadesh. The sources are not silent, however many details of the picture are lacking[117]

114 Guidotti / Pecchioli Daddi 2002.

115 Breyer 2010.

116 On interdynastic marriages see Pintore 1978, in particular 33–45 on the marriages of Ramesses II to Hittite princesses.

117 In particular, there is no clue about the state of the Egyptian-Hittite relations in the treaties, apart from the mention of the about-turn of Aziru, king of Amurru, who was first a subordinate of Egypt and then turned to Ḫatti (CTH 49.II, obv. i 14–29. For a translation see Beckman 1999, 37). On the fleeting alliances of Aziru of Amurru see Devecchi 2012) and a specific clause labelled by G.

and there is no evidence of a direct military confrontation comparable to the Battle of Qadesh.[118]

- Phase 4 = The Battle of Qadesh. This can be considered a phase of its own, although chronologically shorter than the others. Even if it is possible that before the battle Ḫatti and Egypt had more than one conflict, perhaps for the control of some subordinate polities like Amurru, the Battle of Qadesh represents the culminating point of the crisis, since it can be considered a turning point in the Hittite-Egyptian relations, as the sources suggest.
- Phase 5 = The aftermath. For this phase there is an abundance of sources, i.e. the letters exchanged between Ramesses II and Ḫattušili III that, however, do not cover the phase immediate after the Battle of Qadesh and the brief reign of Urḫi-Teššup. The final step of this phase is not the peace treaty that was concluded 15 years after the Battle of Qadesh and that still represents a solid moment in the alliance between Ḫatti and Egypt, but probably the two interdynastic marriages between Ramesses II and two Hittite princesses that consolidated an alliance that remained unbroken as long as the Hittite Empire lasted.

This overview of the phases shows that for the evaluation of the Battle of Qadesh as a culminating point of a crisis, it is important to consider the events before and after the battle and to also sketch, as precisely as possible, the development of the relations between Ḫatti and Egypt. Only in the broader context is it possible to actually attribute to the Battle of Qadesh the definition of a "culminating point" of a crisis.

2.2.4 Asynchronicity at Work

After having discussed the sources and analyzed the information they provide about the facts, as well as having explored different interpretations of the sources, and established how the Battle of Qadesh can be described as a "culminating, decisive point" within a crisis, it is now necessary to delve deeper and put all the different perspectives and perceptions into context. This will help us to understand why this particular crisis was and is viewed asynchronously.

Beckman (1999, 80) "Loyalty against Egypt" in which the king of Amurru Tuppi-Teššub will break the conditions of the treaty if he turns to the king of Egypt.

118 See in general Bryce 2005, 190–220, more specifically Del Monte 1985 and Breyer 2010, 209–213.

The first perspective to be considered is that of the actors directly involved in the events, namely the Hittites and the Egyptians. Based on the sources that we have on the event, these perspectives were asynchronic. In fact, according to the Egyptian sources, the Battle of Qadesh was indeed a pivotal moment that calls for action. Specifically, the Egyptian Pharaoh was required to take action, and since the Egyptian sources describe the battle as a victory for Ramesses II, it is clear that his contemporaries recognized the battle as a defining event that brought an end to the crisis with the Hittites.

The Hittite perspective differs significantly. While there are no surviving sources from the reign of Muwatalli II, the available documents seem to discuss the Battle of Qadesh in various ways.

Firstly, CTH 81 includes a brief report of Ḫattušili's participation in the battle, shifting the focus from the battle itself to Ḫattušili and his military capacity as king of Ḫakpiš. This suggests that the Hittites viewed the Battle of Qadesh as one of many military conflicts, rather than a defining moment of crisis. Furthermore, the letters exchanged between Ramesses II and Hattusili III completely downplay the significance of the battle. They refer to it as the "days of the enemies" without providing any further elaboration.

Unfortunately, since there are no sources dated to the reign of Muwatalli II, the Hittite perspective is asynchronic in respect to the event, and also to some extent with respect to the Egyptian perspective.

The second perspective is that of the neighboring polities, specifically the other players in the "regional system". Unfortunately, we do not have any sources other than the Hittites and the Egyptians that explicitly make reference to the Battle of Qadesh, so our understanding of this viewpoint is limited. On one hand, the absence of any direct references to the conflict between the Hittites and the Egyptians suggests that it may have been seen as a regular instance of hostility between two polities, rather than as an extraordinary event. On the other hand, since the outcome of the battle did not alter the system in a significant way that involved the interests of the neighboring polities, and since the geopolitical situation in the region – the border between the Hittite and Egyptian Empires – remained unchanged, even if the confrontation was seen as a culminating point, it did not have a significant impact on the balance of power in the area.

As far as we can interpret, the perception of the neighboring polities was more aligned with that of the Hittites, and different from that of the Egyptians. However, it is not possible to speculate further about each specific polity. It would make sense to think that the Syro-Levantine polities directly affected by the result of the clash might have perceived the battle as a more decisive moment, not for the system as a whole but only for themselves. On the other hand, other polities less directly involved might have considered the conflict to be unexceptional or not significant for their own interests. However, without sufficient sources, this remains purely speculative.

Finally, we should discuss our perspective as historians. It is important to acknowledge that our perspective is inherently asynchronic due to the time gap between the events we study and the present day. Additionally, our understanding of historical events is shaped by the sources we rely on and how we interpret them, especially when defining certain moments as "crises". In the case of the Battle of Qadesh, two different perspectives need to be considered. If we solely focus on the sources that document the actual showdown, particularly the biased propagandistic Egyptian sources influenced by Ramesses' political agenda, we would perceive the Battle of Qadesh as the culminating point of a crisis between two political entities.

However, there are two additional factors that should be taken into account. First, during the Late Bronze Age, the "regional system" was relatively stable, as none of the "Great Powers' Club" members, the so-called Great Kings, possessed the military or political capacity to subjugate the others. Consequently, any hostility between two of these kings had the potential to upset the balance and alter the geopolitical landscape of the region. Also from this perspective, the Battle of Qadesh can be regarded therefore as a "decisive point", since it was the only open field battle of the period between two Great Kings that had the potential to change the equilibrium in the region, and therefore to shape the political relations after the showdown. Secondly, although Hittite sources are silent regarding the battle itself, there are numerous Hittite texts that provide insight into the period leading up to the Battle of Qadesh, starting from the reign of Šuppiluliuma I.

From the evidence provided by the sources, it is indeed possible to trace "the road to Qadesh", which allows for an understanding of the development of Egyptian-Hittite relations from Šuppiluliuma I until the Battle of Qadesh and beyond. Despite Muršili II issuing several sources to serve his own political agenda, it is clear that the relationship between Ḫatti and Egypt deteriorated during the reigns of Šuppiluliuma I and Muršili II. Although the exact causes of the crisis are not fully documented, it is evident that strained relations developed over time, leading to a series of events that ultimately culminated in the Battle of Qadesh, a decisive moment requiring action.

To sum up, it is possible to conclude that this crisis is linked to three different temporalities: 1. The temporality of the Hittites, who seem to perceive the significance of the Battle of Qadesh only after the clash and in the perspective of the future relations; 2. Our temporality, as historians, which can be divided into two different levels, the Egyptian level that put Qadesh in the center of political and propagandistic agenda, and the Hittite one that seems almost to ignore the clash; and 3. The temporality of the neighboring polities that may have perceived the event as a crisis between Ḫatti and Egypt, but since the battle itself had no consequences on the system, it was not perceived as the culminating point of a crisis, at least not synchronically.

2.3 Case Study #3 The Reign of Ḫattušili III: A Crisis in (Temporal) Disguise

2.3.1 The Milestones of Ḫattušili's Career

In order to understand why the reign of Ḫattušili III is the perfect case study of a crisis that can be defined as an "immanent transitional phase", it is fundamental to trace the main lines of the event that characterized not only Ḫattušili's time as king of Ḫatti but also, maybe even with more attention, what happened before he became king, as well as the picture we can draw from the information in the sources.

I will discuss the sources dating to the time of Ḫattušili III and specifically concerning the crisis more in detail in the next paragraph, but one text, CTH 81,[119] must be examined first here. It is the leading source for the milestones of Hattusili's career and it has been traditionally defined by the scholarship as "Apology".[120] In this long text, whose genre has been not clearly defined by the scholarship and that may have possibly served multiple different purposes,[121] the Hittite king reports, for the sake of his own political and propagandistic agenda, the most important milestones of his career from a very early age to his ascension to the throne as king of Ḫatti in a sort of autobiography. In particular, the text aims to justify his kingship in Ḫatti after he deposed his nephew Urḫi-Teššup.[122] In the next paragraphs I will explain in more detail the definition of the crisis represented by the reign of Ḫattušili, but first, some groundwork is necessary to understand the text. Two lines of reasoning justify Ḫattušili's claim to the throne: a juridical

119 The manuscripts and the studies on CTH 81 can be found here: https://www.hethport.uni-wuerzburg.de/hetkonk/hetkonk_abfrage.php?c=81 (last access 27/01/2025).

120 CTH 81. For the editions and the numerous studies see https://www.hethport.uni-wuerzburg.de/hetkonk/hetkonk_abfrage.php?c=81 (last access 27/01/2025). The *editio princeps* is Otten 1981.

121 According to Laroche 1971, 15 and Hoffner 1980 the text belongs to historiography; Sturtevant and Bechtel in their 1935 edition label the document as "Apology", definition also accepted by Otten 1981 and Hoffner 1975, 49 defines the document "as composed for a king who had usurped the throne, in order to defend or justify his assumption of the kingship by force". The document is defined as decree by Cancik 1970, 65; Archi 1971; Hoffner 1980; Haas 2006, 90. The most recent contribution by de Martino (2023) defines the document as "Apology".

122 See Knapp 2015, 119–160.

one, in which Ḫattušili explains that his motives for deposing Urḫi-Teššup were valid, since Urḫi-Teššup may have broken the clauses of an agreement between the two[123]; and a religious one based upon divine predestination, since Ḫattušili presents himself as chosen – even as a child – by the goddess Ištar to become king.[124] The "autobiography" with its propagandistic and apologetic tones comprises most of the text (obv. i 9 – rev. iv 59) and some specific milestones are narrated with a great deal of detail.

As far as is narrated in the "Apology", the *cursus honorum* of Ḫattušili III presented the following milestones:

- Priest of the Goddess Ištar
- Chief of the Royal Bodyguard
- Governor of the Upper Land
- King of Ḫakpiš
- King of Ḫatti

The transition from king of Ḫakpiš to king of Ḫatti is marked by the most crucial event in the career of Ḫattušili, i. e. his confrontation with Urḫi-Teššup, since Ḫattušili's success in this conflict resulted in Urḫi-Teššup being deposed and the beginning of Ḫattušili's reign in Ḫatti.

It is obvious that the conflict between Ḫattušili and Urḫi-Teššup can be objectively described as a crisis, and more specifically as a dynastic crisis.

However, the analysis of this case study is based on specific research questions that broaden the horizon from just an episode of the civil war between an uncle and nephew for the Hittite throne.

In particular, this analysis is based on the following two questions: 1. Was the conflict perceived as crisis (or, indeed, perceived at all before its outcome) by the neighboring polities? If it was, is it possible to see it in the sources, and how? 2. What is the perception of the scholarship (of us, as historians) of the reign of Ḫattušili III? What has more weight? The narrative of the dynastic crisis or the fact, for instance, that under his reign the "eternal treaty" with Ramesses II was concluded?

Clearly, it is also crucial for this study to understand what the internal Hittite perspective on the reign of Ḫattušili was.

123 See Pallavidini 2017a.

124 Gilan 2022 and Pallavidini forthcoming.

2.3.2 The Sources

The reign of Ḫattušili III can be described as the most well documented reign of a Hittite king in terms of textual sources for two reasons: 1. The sources belong to different textual genres that have different purposes and therefore shed light on specific issues from different perspectives; 2. Among the sources there are texts directed to an international audience, i. e. the other kings and their families, dignitaries, élites, and courtiers, and also texts directed to an internal audience, i. e. the Hittite élites, functionaries and dignitaries, the court, and the royal family.[125]

The texts that can be described as international sources belong specifically to three different textual genres: international treaties, correspondence, and international decrees and verdicts.[126]

In particular, two treaties can be attributed to Ḫattušili III: CTH 92[127], a subordinate treaty concluded with Bentešina, king of Amurru and CTH 91[128], the parity treaty concluded with Pharaoh Ramesses II fifteen years after the Battle of Qadesh.[129]

The international decrees and verdicts have a peculiar characteristic: they were mostly found in Ugarit, and not in Ḫattuša, unlike the rest of the sources, and since they bear the seal impression of the Hittite king their attribution is indubitable. These texts are the decrees CTH 93, CTH 94 (RS 17.238), RS 18.114 (CTH 215), CTH 106.II.1 (ABoT 1.57)[130] and the verdicts RS 17.229 (CTH 215), CTH 95 (RS 17.133).[131]

In contrast with the relatively small number of treaties, international decrees, and verdicts, the letters are particularly abundant, in addition, they were ex-

125 A list of the sources of the reign of Ḫattušili III can be found here: https://www.hethport.uni-wuerzburg.de/CTH/index.php?l=Ḫattušili%20III (last access 27/01/2025).

126 For an overview of these sources during the Hittite Empire see Pallavidini 2016a, *passim*.

127 For an overview of the studies see https://www.hethport.uni-wuerzburg.de/hetkonk/hetkonk_abfrage.php?c=92 (last access 27/01/2025), for an English translation Beckman 1999, 100–103 and for the most recent translation (in Italian) Devecchi 2015, 220–225.

128 See https://www.hethport.uni-wuerzburg.de/hetkonk/hetkonk_abfrage.php?c=91 for the studies concerning this document. The reference edition is Edel 1997, for an English translation see Beckman 1999, 96–100 and for the most recent translation (in Italian) Devecchi 2015, 265–270.

129 It is possible that the treaty with Ulmi-Teššub, king of Tarḫuntašša may also be ascribed to Ḫattušili III. However, the initial part with the name of the Hittite king is missing and the treaty may be also attributed to Ḫattušili's son and successor Tutḫaliya IV. See van den Hout 1995 and, most recently, Devecchi 2015, 160–162.

130 This is the only decree found in Ḫattuša and written in Hittite.

131 For an overview of the Hittite juridical procedures in Syria see D'Alfonso 2005 and, specifically on these texts Pallavidini 2016b.

changed not only with other kings of equal ranks belonging to the so-called Great Powers' Club, but also with subordinate kings, like for instance with the king of Amurru, Bentešina. This is a privileged characteristic of the documentation, since it allows us to see – when possible – different perspectives about what information was communicated to whom and in what form, so that it is also possible to speculate about why specific topics were selected.

Among the letters with other kings of equal rank, the vast majority of the letters dating to the reign of Ḫattušili III were exchanged with Ramesses II and other members of his family,[132] but letters were also exchanged with Babylonia (KBo 1.10+, from Ḫattušili to Kadašman-Enlil; KUB 3.71, from Kadašman-Turgu to Ḫattušili) and, possibly, with Assyria.[133]

The "internal sources" also belong to different genres, however the best preserved are the decrees.[134]

Of course, the longest and best-preserved text is CTH 81, the so-called "Apology" and it is also the document that gives the most insight into and details on the events from the reign of Muwatalli II until Ḫattušili's ascension to the throne of Ḫatti. The scholarship has already pointed out that the document has a propagandistic purpose,[135] with the aim of legitimizing not only Ḫattušili himself but also especially his successor Tutḫaliya, since he was named crown prince (*tuḫkanti*)[136] after his brother Nerikkaili's removal from that position.[137]

The decrees are comprised of six documents and deal with various topics: CTH 85 is very close to the "Apology" and reports the conflict between Ḫattušili and Urḫi-Teššup;[138] CTH 86 is a decree containing dispositions concerning the estate of Arma-Tarḫunta, one of the political adversaries of Ḫattušili who was found guil-

132 Edel 1994.

133 The attribution of most of the letters exchanged with Assyria is debated. See Mora / Giorgieri 2004, *passim* and specifically for an overview 6–7.

134 Some historiographic texts also belong to the sources of the reign of Ḫattušili III, i. e. CTH 82 (the Annals of Ḫattusili III), CTH 83 (report concerning the military campaigns of Šuppiluliuma I), and CTH 84 (report concerning the deeds of Šuppiluliuma I and Muršili II) but unfortunately they are too fragmentary to be discussed here.

135 See the seminal work of Archi 1971, and, recently Pallavidini 2016a, 262–273 with further references.

136 For a recent revision of this title with reference to previous literature see Planelles Orozco 2017.

137 This episode is shortly referred to in the Bronze Tablet, the treaty between Tutḫaliya IV and Kurunta, king of Tarḫuntašša, obv. ii 43–44 (Otten 1988).

138 https://www.hethport.uni-wuerzburg.de/hetkonk/hetkonk_abfrage.php?c=85 (last access 27/01/2025).

ty of sorcery;[139] CTH 87 contains dispositions in favor of the sons of the chief-scribe Mittanamuwa who was in charge of Ḫattuša when the capital was transferred to Tarḫuntašša;[140] CTH 88 outlines the release of the institution of the *ḫekur* of the deity Pirwa from duties; CTH 89 is a decree containing some dispositions concerning the people of the city of Tiliura; finally, CTH 90 disposes the restoration of the sacred city of Nerik.[141]

From this brief survey of the sources, it emerges that their evaluation can be crucial in defining the crisis. In fact, the war between Ḫattušili and Urḫi-Teššup can be defined as a critical moment, but the question that I will try to answer is whether the crisis extended beyond the end of the conflict, and if so, with what consequences, in order to determine whether it is possible to define it as an "immanent transitional phase". To this end, we must sift through a variety of sources which will offer differing perspectives and details on the war. Furthermore, the different sources will shed light on the mechanisms of communication within and around the crisis, in particular, what information was communicated to whom, how it was communicated, and why. One illuminating example concerns the management of Ḫattuša when the capital was transferred to Tarḫuntašša: in CTH 81 Ḫattušili claims that he was governing Ḫattuša (CTH 81, rev. iii 36–37), while, in contrast, in the decree for Mittanamuwa it is stated that Muwatalli selected Mittanamuwa to manage Ḫattuša while the capital was in Tarḫuntašša (CTH 87, obv. 13–19). Further narrative inconsistencies between the different texts arise when the Apology is compared with the decree KBo 6.29+, concerning the priesthood of the goddess Ištar, as is precisely underlined in a recent study by S. de Martino.[142]

2.3.3 The Crisis (or Crises)

As CTH 81 makes evident, the steps toward the conflict between Ḫattušili and Urḫi-Teššup are relatively easy to follow, and they can be summarized in 6 key episodes:

1. rev. iii 36 – rev. ii 54: this section lists the offices of Ḫattušili and Urḫi-Teššup and, in broad terms, their respective spheres of influence.

139 https://www.hethport.uni-wuerzburg.de/hetkonk/hetkonk_abfrage.php?c=86 (last access 27/01/2025).

140 https://www.hethport.uni-wuerzburg.de/hetkonk/hetkonk_abfrage.php?c=87 (last access 27/01/2025).

141 https://www.hethport.uni-wuerzburg.de/hetkonk/hetkonk_abfrage.php?c=88 (last access 27/01/2025).

142 De Martino 2023.

2. rev. iii 54 – rev. iii 62: this short paragraph represents the first moment of hostility, since it reports the first move of Urḫi-Teššub, who takes away from his uncle all the territories subjected to him with the exception of Ḫakpiš and Nerik.
3. rev. iii 63 – rev. iii 79: this section is dedicated to the official and diplomatic preparation of the clash. It is divided into three specific moments: Urḫi-Teššup's removal of Ḫakpiš and Nerik from Ḫattušili; the decision of Ḫattušili to proceed with an actual war; and finally, the declaration of war according to the diplomatic customs of the time, that is, through written communication.
4. rev. iv 1 – rev. iv 23: this part of the narrative focuses on the description of their respective allies, or at least the most significant ones, namely Šipa-Ziti, son of Arma-Tarḫunta who supported Urḫi-Teššup and, on the other side, the goddess Ištar, the Kaška and "the entire Ḫattuša" (rev. iv 28) in favor of Ḫattušili.
5. rev. iv 23 – rev. iv 31: these few lines contain the report of the actual conflict, in which Ḫattušili defeats Urḫi-Teššup.
6. rev. iv 31 – rev. iv 48: the last part of the narrative is dedicated to the consequences of the clash; Urḫi-Teššup is first entrusted with cities in the country of Nuḫašše, but then he is eventually removed from this office, and the properties of his ally Šipa-Ziti are given to the goddess Ištar. As a final but critical consequence of the clash, Ḫattušili becomes Great King of Ḫatti.

However, as already pointed out, the goal of this analysis is not only to evaluate the point of crisis of the open confrontation between Ḫattušili and Urḫi-Teššup, but to determine whether the reign of Ḫattušili III can be interpreted as an immanent transitional phase.

In order to do so, we need to proceed with an analysis of the sources available. In particular, the following questions need to be answered: 1. Are there documents that report the conflict with Urḫi-Teššup, and if so, how do they do it? 2. Are these sources crafted for an international or for an internal audience?

Besides CTH 81, which presents the most detailed narrative concerning the conflict between Ḫattušili and Urḫi-Teššup, another nearly equally detailed narrative about it is presented in KBo 6.29+, obv. i 22 – ii 41). The narrative is consistent with the one in CTH 81, but some significant details are different. Not only is KBo 6.29+ richer in details than CTH 81, but in KBo 6.29+ the impetus of the conflict is attributed to a much more massive intervention of the goddess Ištar.[143]

143 For specific details see de Martino 2023.

These differences might seem minimal, but they are actually crucial in order to understand the political (and propagandistic) agenda of Ḫattušili III, as the decree for Mittanamuwa has already shown.

The other textual category in which Urḫi-Teššup plays a significant role are the letters. In the majority of these documents Urḫi-Teššup is not explicitly mentioned, but the context reveals that the texts refer to him or in general to the conflict between him and Ḫattušili, as for instance in KBo 1.10+, sent by Ḫattušili to Kadašman-Enlil of Babylon, in which we read:

> My enemy who [had escaped] to another country [left] and went to the king of Egypt. When I wrote to him: '[Send me my enemy]', and he did not send me my enemy, [then, because of this, I and the king of] Egypt became angry with one another.[144]

The conflict between Ḫattušili and Urḫi-Teššup surfaces more often in the Hittite-Egyptian correspondence than in any other, with at least eleven letters that mention the conflict.[145] In particular, two letters, KUB 3.22+ (obv. 9) and KBo 1.24+ (*passim*) refer to the "matter of Urḫi-Teššup" and it is clear from the context of both letters that the topic was causing some tensions between Ḫattušili and Ramesses, even if the general tone of the letters maintains the purpose of the good relations.

The analysis of the written sources makes clear that the conflict between Ḫattušili and Urḫi-Teššup is definitely attested more often in the decrees, which were intended for the Hittite audience, and less in the international documents.[146]

The correspondence with Egypt is the most significant exception, however this can be explained by the fact that Urḫi-Teššup found shelter in Egypt and therefore, at least before the conclusion of the treaty between Ramesses II and Ḫattušili III, he could have represented a threat to the good relations between Ḫatti and Egypt, which Ḫattušili wished to maintain in order to bolster the stability of his own power in Ḫatti.[147]

---

144 KBo 1.10+, obv. 66–69. Translation after Beckman 1999, 141.

145 This group of letters has been labelled by V. Cordani "momenti di tensione" (tense moments). See Cordani 2017, 75–96 for more details on the single letters and a translation (in Italian).

146 The conflict between Ḫattušili and Urḫ-Teššup is also narrated in CTH 105, obv. ii 20–38 and in the Bronze Tablet, obv. i 13–17, however these texts are not considered further since they were issued by the successor of Ḫattušili, Tutḫaliya IV for his own poltical agenda. It is however interesting to notice that the episode was still narrated and exploited long after it happened.

147 Ph. Houwink ten Cate dedicated, some time ago, two studies to the "career" of Urḫi-Teššup and to trying to figure out whether some texts could be attributed to this king. Even though some considerations of Houwink ten Cate are now outdated, for an overview about Urḫi-Teššup see Houwink ten Cate 1974 and – for a revision of the topic –1994. For a more recent overview of the reign of Urḫi-Teššup see Bryce 2005, 246–265.

Further evidence emerges from the analysis indicating that the international documents are less rich in details concerning the relationship and the ultimate conflict between Ḫattušili and Urḫi-Teššup. However, the texts for the internal audience always report roughly the same general narrative, so it is possible to say that the internal documents are richer in details, as well as consistently providing the same version of the events.

This difference plays a significant role in perceptions of the crisis. The international audience, who could probably only speculate about the actual events that caused Urḫi-Teššup to be deposed, perceived the crisis of the time *post quem*, and their perception of the crisis was focused on the fact that Urḫi-Teššup had survived and that his presence in Egypt presented a continued threat to stability.

The internal audience, in contrast, probably had direct knowledge of the major events of the confrontation that went beyond the narrative of the sources. Additionally, they must have perceived the conflict as occurring over a longer period time, beginning with the events leading up to the conflict between Ḫattušili and Urḫi-Teššup and continuing into the aftermath of the conflict. This can be determined from the presence of attempts at justification in the texts of Ḫattušili, and even though the narrative within the text itself ends with Ḫattušili becoming king of Ḫatti, the same narrative is present in texts that were written long after the confrontation, for example, the "Apology", which was composed after the deposition of Nerikkaili as *tuḫkanti* (crown prince).[148]

This analysis allows us to draw a further conclusion, which is that it is clear there was a three-fold crisis that stretched over a period of time longer than the actual reign of Ḫattušili III.

The first crisis point, before Ḫattušili became king in Ḫatti, was the confrontation with Urḫi-Teššup and all its consequences, two of which should be mentioned in particular. The first is Tarḫuntašša's loss of its status as capital and therefore it had to be decided what to do with it. The second was the presence of Urḫi-Teššup, Muwatalli's other family members, in Egypt and of his political supporters in Ḫatti.

This second element is closely connected with the second "crisis-point" that is not a specific event, but rather the whole issue of legitimation. Since Ḫattušili had no real claim to the throne of Ḫatti, and since the way he took power as king was questionable, not only was his hold on the throne unstable, but the succession of his heirs was also uncertain.

The third and final crisis-point concerns the stability of Ḫattušili's power on an international level. The Battle of Qadesh was fought not long before he ascend-

148 See Imparati 1995.

ed to the throne and, in particular, not long before his conflict with Urḫi-Teššup. The turmoil in Ḫatti might have weakened the power of Ḫattušili on an international level and caused the rebellion of the subordinate kings, as well as emboldening Egypt to attempt to acquire more territories in Syria.

The fact that these situations were perceived to be the expression of an ongoing crisis or as potentially leading up to a crisis, at least by Ḫattušili, and also probably by the Hittite audience, is demonstrated by the fact that some measures were taken as possible solutions.

The first and most obvious is, as already described, the attempts to justify the actions of Ḫattušili by using the narrative of the texts to establish an official version of events.

However, more concrete anti-crisis measures can also be detected. First, as pointed out by F. Imparati, the decrees present not only a specific apologetic narrative but also contain concrete and specific economic measures aimed at placating institutions and dignitaries with the purpose of currying favor toward Ḫattušili.[149]

The crisis initiated by the transfer of the capital to Ḫattuša from Tarḫuntašša was addressed together with the possible crisis connected with the presence of living family members of Muwatalli II: as is well known, Tarḫuntašša was made a *Sekundogenitur* (as Karkemiš had been before) with the enthronement of Kurunta, a son of Muwatalli, as king.[150]

The critical issue of legitimation was dealt with in the narrative in CTH 81 with two lines of justification: a juridical one, according to which Urḫi-Teššup violated the terms of an agreement with Ḫattušili, and a religious one in which the goddess Ištar is described as having predestined Ḫattušili for the throne of Ḫatti.

The legitimation of Tutḫaliya is accomplished by the texts, in particular by CTH 81, not by a narrative of Ḫattušili's predestination, but by the very specific measure of appointing him as priest of the goddess Ištar, having him reenact one of the first steps of Ḫattušili's career.

The third and final critical issue, the stability of Ḫattušili's power in international relations, was tackled by a diplomatic program, through the exchange of a dense correspondence with Egypt that had as its first goal the stipulation of a treaty, and as its ultimate goal the acquisition of a powerful ally. Furthermore, the sources include very detailed diplomatic letters exchanged with other kings, like the one sent to Kadašman-Enlil, in which the Hittite king tackles several different

149 Imparati 1988.
150 See Sürenhagen 1992 and D'Alfonso 2014 on the assessment of the political role of Tarḫuntašša.

topics, including relations with other countries such as Egypt and Assyria, good diplomatic practices, and more specific subjects like the murder of some Hittite merchants or the situation of Bentešina, king of Amurru.[151] These letters are a specific sign of the will of Ḫattušili III to stabilize and strengthen his position in the Great Powers' Club, and with the subordinate kings for the control of satellite polities.

To return to the fundamental question of whether the reign of Ḫattušili can be considered "an immanent transitional phase", I think it is possible to answer affirmatively. The crisis-points from the confrontation with Urḫi-Teššup to the succession of Tutḫaliya IV could have triggered several changes and realignments, for instance a change in the reigning family in Ḫatti, as had happened before,[152] a shift in power in favor of Tarḫuntašša and its royal family, and the breakdown of relations with Egypt or with other members of the Great Powers' Club. However, none of this happened, and the crisis (or crises) was indeed a transitional phase from the reign of one branch of the royal family to another, from the initial intention of good relations with Egypt to the actual stipulation of a treaty, and from rocky successions to the stability of the reign of both Ḫattušili and his son Tutḫaliya as ensured by the conclusion of his treaty with his cousin Kurunta.[153]

2.3.4 Asynchronicity in Disguise

Defined as an immanent transitional period, the reign of Ḫattušili III can no longer be described without question as the apogee of the Hittite Empire. The stipulation of a treaty with Egypt and the fact that the international sources give us a picture of stability and power in international relations are consistent with the idea of the reign of Ḫattušili as being the apogee of the Hittite political power, before the crisis that would bring it to an end became manifest. However, the dynastic crisis and the measures taken to ensure the stability of Ḫattušili's power within Ḫatti show how his reign was a transition between the reign of his predecessors Šuppiluliuma, Muršili, and Muwatalli and the reign of his descendants. However, since the crisis was perceived as largely internal to Ḫatti, in this case study the asynchronic perception of the crisis also plays an important role, even if it disguises itself in the synchronic sources available.

151 KBo 1.10+: https://www.hethport.uni-wuerzburg.de/hetkonk/hetkonk_abfrage.php (last access 27/01/2025). For the translation of the letter see Beckman 1999, 138–143.

152 See case study #1 in Ch. 2.1.

153 The most recent recap of the possible conspiracy of Kurunta against Tutḫaliya is the article of Arroyo, forthcoming, with the discussion of the previous literature.

The first temporality is that of the Hittites. Their perspective on the crisis is the only one synchronic with it, since as the sources reveal, the narrative of the texts, as well as the texts themselves, are witnesses to the ongoing crisis, representing measures to address and possibly resolve it. In this case what is asynchronic is that the goal of the anti-crisis measures was not to resolve critical issues in the reign of Ḫattušili, but rather to prevent further crises in the reign of Ḫattušili's successor(s).

The perspective of the neighboring polities is for the most part asynchronic, since the crisis was mostly internal to Ḫatti, and the international sources, with the exception of the letters mentioning Urḫi-Teššup, do not describe the issues of the crisis. Indeed, the international sources do not show any concern from the kings of the neighboring polities regarding the situation in Ḫatti. Considering that the reign of Ḫattušili is defined as a transitional phase, the most asynchronic perception is our own. As a matter of fact, a transitional phase implies that a certain period of time has passed before it can be perceived as such, and both the Hittite and their neighbors were within the same temporality of the crisis and could not, therefore, have perceived the transition. Since historians are in a different temporality and can evaluate the totality of the sources available, we are able to perceive the immanent transitional phase and to describe the changes and the transformations that it brought with it.

2.4 Case Study #4 The End of the Hittite Empire: Asynchronic Synchronicity

2.4.1 The End of an Era

Fall. Collapse. End. The period between the end of the 13th and the beginning of the 12th century BCE and the corresponding passage from the Late Bronze Age to the Iron Age, has been described with all these words by the scholarship, often together with demise and decline.[154]

These different terms imply different views of the period they describe. The most neutral term is "end" and it often refers simply to the Hittite empire or, more precisely, to the end of the written documentation from Ḫattuša. Both references to an "end" are in fact correct: the Hittite empire ceased to exist – at least in the form that was known in the Late Bronze Age – and its end, along with other factors, catalyzed the re-organization of the "regional system" that also ceased to

154 For more details about these definitions, see below.

exist in the form it took in the Late Bronze Age.[155] The assumption that the Hittite Empire ended is due to the fact that written sources from Ḫattuša are no longer available after the reign of Šuppiluliuma II who is, at the current state of the research, the last known Hittite king.[156]

The other two terms, "fall" and "collapse", are definitely far less neutral than "end" but not necessarily incorrect.[157]

They both imply the end not only of the written sources and of a known dynasty of kings, but also of the social, political, and economic structures that characterized the Hittite Empire.

J. Diamond defines collapse as "a drastic decrease in human population size and/or political/economic/social complexity, over a considerable area, for an extended time",[158] underlining different aspects and implying that collapse is a complex phenomenon, caused by different factors and extended over time, meaning that it does not happen suddenly. However, regarding the Hittite Empire specifically, L. D'Alfonso defines collapse as a "rapid and deep political change", underlining the quickness of the change but also the fact that, as he states more precisely, "collapse never means the complete end of political systems and their accompanying civilizational frameworks"[159], thus already pointing toward the use of concepts like re-organization, transformation, or simply change to better describe the situation after the end of written documentation from Ḫattuša.

Fall is often used as synonym of collapse, referring traditionally to a multifactorial complex set of causes that led to the end of a polity and its political structures, and it is often connected with the concept of "decline" that is the phase – of crisis – that precedes the fall.[160]

These definitions also link the end of an empire (or of a civilization) with the factors that determined it.

While the most recent research tends to point out the multifactoriality of the causes that determine the end of an empire, in this regard scholarship's interpretation of the end of Hittite Empire has changed dramatically in the last decade.

It is beyond the purpose of this study to retrace the whole history of research concerning the fall of the Hittite Empire[161] but a change seems to have occurred in the interpretation of the scholarship, moving from a monocausal explanation for

155 See Liverani 2013, 381–400.
156 See de Martino 2022a, 255–259. On the reign of Šuppiluliuma II see Bryce 2005, 327–356.
157 The term "collapse" is used a.o. by de Martino 2022b.
158 Diamond 2005, 3.
159 D'Alfonso 2020, 97.
160 See recently Gehler *et al.* (eds.) 2022, 1–45.
161 On this topic see recently Alaura 2020.

the end of the Hittite Empire (usually related to the invasion of the Sea People or of other groups), to the highlighting of internal factors of decline (like depopulation and famine).[162] There are two specific reevaluations in the scholarship that should be mentioned here: the one suggested by J. Seeher, who first suggested that the end of the written documentation from Ḫattuša should be interpreted not as caused by a catastrophic event, but rather as the consequence of the abandonment of the capital by the Hittites themselves, as based on archaeological evidence.[163] The second reevaluation is the rise of the "resilience theory" that not only presupposes that a plethora of causes must have determined the end of the Empire, but also that treats the end itself as nuanced, interpreting it more as a re-organization and change rather than of destruction and oblivion.[164]

If, on the one hand, it is true that the written documentation from Ḫattuša ceased, and that after Šuppiluliuma II there was no known king who bore the title of "King of Ḫatti" and that the sequence indeed broke off, on the other hand, the definition of what happened in the period leading to the end of the Hittite Empire and in its aftermath is should be interpreted as something like re-organization and resilience.[165]

The truth is that we do not know with certainty what happened to the Hittite royal dynasty after the abandonment of the capital, but definitions like fall or collapse seem improper to some degree.

Most probably, the end of the written sources and of the sequence of kings was not caused by a single sudden catastrophic event or by a series of intertwined catastrophic events in a domino-like-effect. It was the result of a series of causes, none of which can be defined as sudden or catastrophic.

In S. Alaura's excellent definition:

> regarding the actual cause of the "crisis" at the end of the Late Bronze Age, recent suggestions include: destruction by outside forces (…) climate and environmental changes or natural disasters (…) technological innovations (…) internal collapse (…) and anthropological and sociological theories dealing with states of inequalities and the resulting political struggle.[166]

After having defined the characteristics of the end of the Hittite Empire and its causes, we must now examine the sources that inform us about the critical scenario that led to the fall. Furthermore, the question of the definition of the crisis

---

162 Singer 1985 and 2000.

163 Seeher 2001 and 2010.

164 See Faulseit (ed.) 2016 and Middleton 2017.

165 For an overview from the archaeological perspective see Manuelli 2016.

166 Alaura 2020, 20.

remains open, and, in particular, it must be decided whether the crisis that led to the end of the Hittite Empire can be defined as “a unique and final point”.

2.4.2 The Sources

Surveying the sources related to the end of the Hittite Empire is particularly complex for two reasons.

First, since archaeological sources are crucial for the reconstruction of the fall and its aftermath, they must be taken into consideration, but with the caveat that they often draw a picture different from the one drawn by the written sources, and this can also be seen as a point of asynchronicity.[167]

Second, there is no source that is an explicit report of the crisis or that explicitly mentions Hittite fear of the changes that were taking place, so we have to read between the lines of the texts in order to catch references to the crisis or to the Hittite’s fear of the end of the world as they knew it.

As we try to read between the lines, the leading question is of course: did they see it coming? But a follow up question is also necessary: if they did, what measures did they take to deal with it? Were they successful? Or did they only think that they were successful?

The answer to both questions is biased by the availability of the sources. Not only must a certain randomness in the finding of the sources must be taken into consideration, but it is also impossible to exclude the possibility that the Hittite dynasty continued its existence somewhere else, and that it produced written records that have simply not been found (yet). Therefore, the picture we obtain from the sources we have currently might be incomplete.

In a recent contribution, J. Miller answers the question about whether the texts display evidence of the crisis that led to the end of the Hittite Empire by stating “in short: No, there are no signs, or at least no clear signs, of the decline and impending collapse in the documentation from Ḫattuša”.[168] However, he also points out that the scholarship has had radically different opinions on the matter, and underlining in particular the interpretation of I. Singer of the oath and instructions texts of the last Hittite kings as containing references to the decline of the Hittite Empire, and considering the issuing of the documents themselves as measures against the crisis.[169]

167 See below, Ch. 2.4.3.
168 Miller 2020, 237.
169 Singer 1985.

Miller also points out a further significant issue, which is the date of the documents that are sources for the crisis years at the end of the Empire. This is particularly interesting issue, since opinions concerning the timing of the collapse may vary, as shown in the previous paragraph. Therefore, not only is it crucial to delimit the period in which it is possible to find documents that contain references not just to "a crisis" but to "the crisis" that led to the end of the Empire. It is also crucial to have a precise paleographic date of the documents, since as Miller shows, for instance the text Bo 2810 on which, among others, Klengel's interpretation of the hunger in Ḫatti was based[170], dates to the middle of the 13th century BCE and not to the last years of the Empire, therefore the document may indeed contain evidence of a difficult time, but not evidence of the crisis that caused the end of the Empire.

This also implies that it is necessary to set a date for the beginning of the decline, but doing so is a very tricky task. In fact, not only does it depend on the interpretation of the reign of Ḫattušili III, in particular on the evaluation of his reign as the beginning of the crisis that led to the fall of the Empire, but also it depends on what factors of the crisis are taken into consideration as relevant causes of the fall. It is evident that the dynastic crisis marked the reign of Ḫattušili III and had consequences that affected the reign of his successor Tutḫaliya IV at a minimum.[171] However, references to other crisis factors, like drought, hunger, depopulation, conflicts, and so on, are not necessarily present in the written documentation and therefore the beginning of the multifactorial crisis cannot be dated with high precision. Also, the eruption of the different crisis factors might have been asynchronous, so a starting point is impossible to establish.

Finally, as Miller correctly describes it,

> the cluster of documentation during the middle of the 13th century might well mislead us in general, too, in that we are able to find some 10 times as many difficulties and negative events in them, simply because we have 10 times as many texts.[172]

So, the question remains: what texts do we have that contain clues and/or references to the crisis? Is it possible to identify some of these references?

A complete study of the documents of the late Hittite Empire that contain indications of the crisis goes beyond the scope of this research, but I will nevertheless here discuss some texts that have been always considered by the scholarship to be related to the crisis that led to the end of the Empire.

---

170 Klengel 1974.

171 See case study #3 in Ch. 2.3.

172 Miller 2020, 242.

As will become clear in the survey, most of the texts were not written in Ḫattuša but in Ugarit.

The first document that I want to discuss is the letter RS 17.247 sent from Piḫawalwi from Ḫatti to Ibiranu. In the third paragraph of this very short letter we read:

> Why have you not come before His Majesty since you became king in the land of Ugarit? Why have you not sent your messengers? His Majesty is very angry about this matter. So send your messengers to His Majesty quickly and send presents to the king together with presents also for me.[173]

In the words of Piḫawalwi a certain discontent with the behavior if Ibiranu is tangible, since it was probably contrary to the etiquette of diplomacy, and in particular contrary to the expected behavior of a subordinate king toward his overlord at the time of his own accession to the throne. However, certain misbehaviors on the part of the subordinate kings are not exceptional, as the case of Aziru of Amurru shows, and they did not necessarily mean the beginning of hostilities or, even worse, of open confrontation. The words of Piḫawalwi do not conceal any concern for a degenerating situation or fear of an irreversible crisis caused by the behavior of Ibiranu, only irritation and disappointment at Ibiranu's neglect of his duties as subordinate.

If these political interactions do not seem far from regular diplomacy, with a few more tense situations, but without potentially catastrophic changes of alliance and/or confrontations, the topic of food supply is also present in some documents and seems to be a reason for worry. In the letter RS 20.212, as a matter of fact, we read:

> And so (the city of) Ura [acted(?)] in such a way… and for My Sun the food they have saved. My Sun has shown them 2,000 *kor* of grain coming from Mukish. You must furnish them with a large ship and a crew, and they must transport this grain to their country. They will carry it in one or two shipments. You must not detain their ship! (RS 20.212, 17–26)[174]

The wording of the letter, in particular the reference in the very final line to the fact that "it is a matter of life or death" (RS 20.212, line 33), may imply a current problem with a shortage of food, resulting in hunger, and therefore an irreversible crisis.

---

173 Translation by Hoffner 2003a, 53.

174 Translation by Heltzer 1977, 209. For a more recent translation of the letter (in German) see Schwemer 2006b, 258–260.

However, as has already been pointed out by H. A. Hoffner, there is no mention of an imminent catastrophe,[175] therefore even if the wording might seem a little dramatic, it does not necessarily mean that it was actually a matter of life and death, but might rather have been a way to communicate urgency and encourage the recipient to stick to the shipment agreement.

We need also to keep in mind M. Liverani's interpretation of Rib-Addu's correspondence with the Egyptian Pharaoh, where he sees in the constant pleas of Rib-Addu, who describes himself surrounded by enemies and in constant danger, a literary *topos* rather than actual reality.[176]

Since one of the causes of the demise of the Hittite Empire might have been the resource drain of conducting military campaigns against multiple enemies, one of the most interesting texts for our purposes is RS 34.165, because it concerns military operations and hostilities involving the Hittites .[177]

I. Singer has pointed out that the sender and the addressee are not known, however the latter might be Ibiranu, king of Ugarit, and the former Tukultī-Ninurta I, king of Assyria.[178] The letter has been often described as exceptional because it reports actual hostility – possibly including a military confrontation in Niḫriya – between Assyria and Ḫatti. It is rare to find such reports in letters but, as pointed out by D. Schwemer "Ziel des Briefes war es wohl, den König von Ugarit, der ja ein Vasall des Hethiterkönigs war, davon zu überzeugen, das die Macht des Hethiterreiches ihren Zenit überschritten hatte",[179] therefore the hostility between Ḫatti and Assyria, even if it definitely occurred, did not play an actual role in the end of the Hittite Empire and the actual consequences of the military confrontation were not devastating for the Hittites. As I. Singer underlines after reviewing the sources for the last decades of the Hittite history in his detailed article on the battle of Niḫriya: "*Nota bene:* There is nothing in these documents of the last years of the Hittite Empire even remotely associated with the Assyrians or with eastern campaigns",[180] thus downplaying the significance of the hostility as one of the causes of the end of the Hittite Empire.

If we turn to the Hittite internal documents, KBo 12.38 may be the Hittite counterpart of the letter about the battle of Niḫriya.[181] This historiographic text, dated to the reign of Šuppiluliuma II, is – in its second part (obv. ii 22–rev. iv 14) – a

175 Hoffner 1992.
176 Liverani 1974.
177 https://www.hethport.uni-wuerzburg.de/hetkonk/hetkonk_abfrage.php (last access 27/01/2025).
178 See Singer 1985 and Schwemer 2006a, 254.
179 Schwemer 2006a, 254.
180 Singer 1985, 123.
181 https://www.hethport.uni-wuerzburg.de/hetkonk/hetkonk_abfrage.php (last access 27/01/2025).

boastful report of the military successes of the Hittite king against Alašiya, as stated in obv. ii 5–9:

> Ships of the land of Alasiya met me in battle three times on the high seas. I defeated them. I captured the ships and set fire to them in the sea.[182]

Like letter RS 34.165, which had the goal of convincing the king of Ugarit to support Assyria since the Hittite king was not powerful anymore, KBo 12.38, written in a similar tone, is an attempt to convince the Hittite élites and the court that the king was more powerful than their enemies, and that he was able to conquer more subordinates. Furthermore, since the first part of the text deals with the building of a mausoleum to celebrate his father Tutḫaliya (IV) as proclaimed by the words:

> I built a permanent mausoleum. I made the statue and had it carried into the permanent mausoleum (obv. ii 17–21),[183]

a further goal of Šuppiluliuma II was probably to propagate an image of himself as a pious king. Both arguments of the text can be read as measures to reframe a crisis, of power on the international scene in the first case and dynastic in the second, but this way of reframing crises is not unknown in the Hittite Empire, as shown by the cases of Telipinu and Ḫattušili, and the wording of the text does not convey the urgency of a potential catastrophic situation; it is, rather, business as usual for the Hittite kings.

Further evidence that the situation was under control – or at least perceived as such – is given by the treaties of Šuppiluliuma II, one with Talmi-Teššup king of Karkemiš (CTH 122.1)[184] and the other with Alašiya (CTH 141).[185] Both treaties are fragmentary and they show some different characteristics from the treaties of the previous kings.[186] However, they also show the usual features of Hittite international treaties, such as the "motivation clause" (the so-called historical prologue)[187] and the binding obligation to be loyal to the terms of the agreement, as well as the usual terminology attested in the treaties.

---

182 Translation by Hoffner 2003b, 193.
183 Translation by Hoffner 2003b, 193.
184 https://www.hethport.uni-wuerzburg.de/hetkonk/hetkonk_abfrage.php (last access 27/01/2025).
185 https://www.hethport.uni-wuerzburg.de/hetkonk/hetkonk_abfrage.php (last access 27/01/2025).
186 Pallavidini 2017b.
187 This terminology is traditionally used to describe a structural part of the Roman decrees (often in the form of monumental letters) for communities and cities in Asia Minor, and it refers

In particular, it is interesting that CTH 122.1 was concluded between Šuppiluliuma II and the king of Karkemiš. Since the scholarship agrees on the rising role of Karkemiš in the last period of the Hittite Empire, in particular concerning the control and administration of the Syrian subordinate kingdoms,[188] the presence of the treaty represents evidence that Karkemiš was still considered to be and treated like a subordinate kingdom by the Hittites, although still with its status of *Sekundogenitur.*[189]

Finally, surveying the oaths of Ḫattušili III, Tutḫalia IV, and Šuppiluliuma II, M. Giorgieri notices that they tend to emphasize the need for loyalty, for example, as in CTH 124, rev. iii 8–15 in which we read:

> May my years and my days be offered to Šuppil[uliyama]! Whatever happens I will protect only the descendants of my Lord Šuppilu[lium]a, of Muršili, of Muwatalli [and] (?) of Tutḫaliya. I will not speak thus: "That (is) of the oath!" I will protect only the descendants of my Lord!".[190] He also points out that "as the monarchy became weaker, Hittite kings responded by claiming closer intimacy with the gods.[191]

Both the emphasis on loyalty and closeness to the gods may be considered measures to reframe the dynastic crisis initiated by the usurpation of Ḫattušili III. However, in this case also the texts do not convey – at least not convincingly – fear of an imminent end.

As has been shown by the survey of the sources, there is no text that can be defined as explicit about the impending fall of the Empire or even about a general crisis felt to be irreversible.

Different texts deal with different issues, but these issues were also fairly common in previous periods of Hittite history, and it would be a stretch to interpret these passages as evidence of a crisis that was perceived as worse than the previous ones or any that had recurred during Hittite history.

It is also striking that the situation is never described as specifically critical, either by the internal documents or by the international texts like letters. This can indeed be interpreted as evidence that the critical time was not thought to be a leadup to catastrophic consequences.

---

to the description of the reason that led to the decision(s) issued by the decree. See, for an overview, most recently Jordan 2023.

188 See recently D'Alfonso 2011.

189 On the *Sekundogenitur* see Sürenhagen 1992.

190 Giorgieri 2020, 169.

191 Giorgieri 2020. 156.

Based on the textual evidence, it is clear that we must avoid the tendency to make *post eventum* prophecies based solely on our knowledge of the subsequent historical events, i.e. that the regional system did indeed fall.

2.4.3 Asynchronic Synchronicity

After having surveyed the most relevant written sources and having made some comments regarding the end of the Hittite Empire, the question of whether the crisis that led to the end of the documentation from Ḫattuša could be perceived as a "unique and final point" needs to be answered.

As we have done for the previous three case studies, we must consider how this crisis was perceived by the three different perspectives that have been considered throughout this work, specifically, the perspective of the Hittites, the perspective of the neighboring polities, and our perspective as historians, as well as the different temporalities of these perspectives.

In this case there is unique advantage from our sources – at least for the sake of this study – since they derive not only from the Hittite capital but also, perhaps even for the most part, from Ugarit. This circumstance allows the possibility of grasping the perspective of the neighboring polities much more deeply than was the case in the other three case studies.

The perspective of the Hittites has already been described and – as far as it is possible to interpret from the sources available – it is safe to say that, even though some critical issues were perceived (like drought and the consequent scarcity of grain, the movement of people, depopulation, and possibly even some turbulence on an international level), the sources show that the Hittites never really considered the possibility that their Empire could fall. In this context it is necessary to ask a further question: did they not consider this possibility because they did not perceive the gravity of the signals of the crisis, or because what we understand as fall or collapse was not a concept with which they were familiar? It is, of course, impossible to know for sure, as well as beyond the purpose of this research to give even a speculative answer to this question, however this issue is directly linked to asynchronicity as we compare the perspective of the Hittites to our own.

Not only is our temporality different from that of the Hittites, and not only do we have knowledge of what happened after the Hittite Empire ended and the regional system ceased to exist, but the scholarship has used (and still uses) concepts like collapse and fall that are contemporary and therefore convey our perspective.

The consequence is that the scholarship described (and still describes) these concepts according to its own perception, while from an emic perspective they might be perceived in a significantly different way.

This does not mean that the perspective of the scholarship is incorrect, since thanks to our different temporality, we can evaluate these historical events in light of the result of the crisis, i. e. the fall of the Hittite Empire. However, it is important to divide the crisis itself from its results and consequences and, the definition of "unique and final point" can be given only in retrospect and from an etic perspective.

Finally, the perspective of the neighboring polities is in sync with that of the Hittites, since they shared both the same temporality and the same infosphere. The sources do not point out specific concerns of the other Great Kings and/or of the subordinate polities. These might very well have been present, but since all the actors involved in the regional system shared a common cultural environment, is conceivable that their perception of the crisis was very close to that of the Hittites.

To conclude, in this case study the different temporality is the trigger of the asynchronic perception of the crisis, with a significant split between the emic and the etic perspectives.

3 Conclusions: Asynchonicity and (Re)-interpretation of Crises

3.1 Crisis: Temporality vs Perception

After having presented the four case studies and having shown how (a)synchronic these three different perspectives were and whether and how multitemporality plays a role, it is now possible to draw some concluding remarks.

First, it is always important to consider from which perspective a crisis is evaluated. This is not only a simple matter of emic versus etic perspective, but the infosphere,[192] i. e., the sources available to the actors involved, also plays a significant role, and must therefore always be considered when describing and evaluating a crisis. In Hittite history, not only are the sources are partial and incomplete on the one side, and at least partially biased on the other, but different actors – or to put it more precisely, different perspectives – have different access to the sources. This produces asynchronicity not only between the perspective of historians and that of the ancient actors, but also between the Hittites and the neighboring polities, since they also had differing access to multiple sources.

This was evident in the case of the Battle of Qadesh, where the Egyptian audience was overloaded with the Ramesside propaganda, while the impact of the event and its narrative was definitely less significant on the Hittite audience, who was probably more involved in the aftermath.

Second, a crisis may not necessarily been perceived synchronically across the different perspectives and/or by the actors involved in it, and this was dependent not only on access to the sources, as already pointed out, but also on the type of crisis. A good example here are the crises that can be described as transitional, as was shown in the case studies of the reign of Ḫattušili III and the end of the Hittite Empire.

While it is true that any crisis can be considered transitional, since there is always necessarily a before and an after for any event occurring in time, these specific crises are transitional on a longer temporal scale, and they are slower in their unfolding and their effects. These, therefore, are the characteristics that allow us to define the category of transitional crises.

However, for crises that are more punctuated, or have as an apical moment of crisis a specific event, as for instance in the cases of the succession to the throne or the Battle of Qadesh, access to the sources was a more significant factor and deter-

192 See fn. 32.

 https://doi.org/10.1515/9783111712383-005

mined how the involved actors perceived (or did not perceive) the crisis. A further element to consider is also the purpose and the intended audience of the sources, since these influenced perceptions of the crisis as well.

The reign of Ḫattušili III represents a good example of this phenomenon, since the audience who had access to the internal sources was very different from the one that had access to the international ones. In this case, the sources are the potential trigger for asynchronicity across all perspectives, since they interpreted the dynastic crisis to the internal audience, presented a strong and stable international power to the neighboring polities, and at least on a first glance, presented to modern historians the idea that the reign of Ḫattušili III represented the apogee of the Empire.

Finally, we must turn to the relation between (a)synchronicity and multitemporality.

In the majority of the cases the two factors run parallel, but in some cases uneven access to different types of sources can result in asynchronic phenomena surfacing even within the same temporal frame, as we have seen for the reign of Ḫattušili III and also, at least in part, for the Battle of Qadesh.

This is a factor that influences all the case studies, depending partially on the bias of the sources and partially on their accessibility. The phenomenon is also influenced by the type of the crisis and by how the actors who hold the different perspectives are involved.

How a crisis should be categorized varies depending on different perspectives, and the categorization used here is clearly rooted in an etic standpoint. However, my evaluations of the crises are based on the sources available, therefore, my hope is that the data have been correctly interpreted, and my goal has been to evaluate each crisis in a way that is as close as possible to the emic perspective.

This consideration prompts reflection on ancient actors understood crises. In their world, changes often occurred and were perceived on a much longer time scale than today, yet changes on shorter temporal scales were also constantly present. This distinction influences the concept of crisis and, even more so, the factors identified as critical. Conflict was pervasive and often mitigated by diplomacy, while drought, famine, and depopulation were generally viewed as more significant triggers of potentially catastrophic crises. Moreover, the consequences of a crisis also shaped its definition: is a crisis something that radically transforms the known world, or is it a transitional phase that induces changes without producing drastic consequences? As we have observed, the definition of crisis is highly flexible, and we cannot ascertain how the Hittites might have defined it.

From the sources we can reconstruct, there is a sensitivity to critical periods, particularly regarding the case of the dynastic crisis that began with Ḫattušili III, and in the case of Telipinu and the regulation of the succession to the throne. However, the Battle of Qadesh and the final years of the empire are not presented – either implicitly or explicitly – in terms of crisis, especially not as an imminent catastrophic crisis.

It is now necessary to return to the concepts that represent the pillars of this study: (a)synchronicity and crisis.

As the case studies have shown, these two concepts are strongly intertwined. In particular, temporal frames together with access to the sources determined the perceptions of the crisis, and specifically its asynchronicity or its synchronicity across the three perspectives. In turn, the synchronic or asynchronic perception of the crisis from the three different perspectives determines how the crisis is evaluated, and this evaluation can differ significantly among the three perspectives, regardless of whether they share the same temporal frame or not.

3.2 Re-interpreting Crisis in Hittite History

Since the concept of (a)synchronicity and crisis, as well as their connection, have been explored, it is now time to draw some more specific conclusions from the four case studies and the type of crises that they represent, and to try – if possible – to (re)-evaluate them.

In the case of the "Proclamation" of Telipinu the crisis, the recurring critical moment of the succession to the throne, seems to have been perceived synchronically by all actors involved. However, the text might lead to an incorrect interpretation of such a crisis, that it might have been indeed perceived, at least by some actors, asynchronically.

The second case study, the Battle of Qadesh, can be interpreted differently after the evaluation of the sources available, their purpose, and also after having considered the role of asynchronicity.

The clash itself, as well as its immediate consequences, did not change the political scenario of the regional system in the Late Bronze Age. As has been shown, the battle represents the culminating point of a crisis that began long before it. However, its centrality as event for the history of the Ancient Western Asia is likely less important than historians and in general our contemporaries usually perceive. In this case, in fact, the evaluation of the sources causes a reevaluation of the Battle of Qadesh as a significant yet not exceptional conflict between two polities.

The reign of Ḫattušili III is probably the most complex case study to reevaluate, since the sources were predominantly created by the scribes of Ḫattušili III himself, therefore there are few other sources with which to compare them. Furthermore, since the reign of Ḫattušili III has traditionally been thought to represent the apogee of the Hittite Empire, probably because of the conclusion of the peace treaty with Egypt, interpreting it as a transitional crisis is something that must be supported by the sources. Indeed, they reveal a duality: on the one hand, they clearly show the internal dynastic crisis that resulted in consequences that lasted through the reigns of Ḫattušili's successors; on the other hand, the sources also show a great degree of stability in the international relations, despite some tensions related to the presence of Urḫi-Teššup in Egypt.

The reign of Ḫattušili III represents a very good example of the fact that it is often problematic to define a period simply as a crisis, it is also necessary to define the type of crisis, or, in other words, from which perspective it can be considered a crisis.

The last case study, the end of the Hittite Empire, shows possibly the highest degree of asynchronicity between the ancient temporality and perspectives and ours. However, it also represents a paradigmatic example of how the scholarship reevaluated the sources available and has already reinterpreted this period. The multifactorial difficulties that caused the end of the Hittite Empire and of the regional system can be considered a crisis as a unique and final point, since there was a change in the social and political structures and in the economic networks. However, the focus of the most recent scholarship is not on the end itself but on the causes of the changes and on the elements of continuity. This aligns our perspective more synchronously with that of the ancient actors, despite the different temporal frames.

To conclude, it is important to reiterate that our perspective is always etic, meaning we are the ones who define a "crisis" as such. However, it is essential to define the term crisis and, as we have seen, there are different types of crises that can be defined and described on the basis of the available sources. The fundamental question is therefore not so much whether a period can be considered a crisis, but what type of crisis it is, and what the sources say about it. The ultimate goal in answering this question is to bring our perspectives as close as possible to that of the ancient actors or, at least, to understand their (often) different perspectives. By doing this it is possible to reduce the inconsistencies produced by asynchronicity and to gain a better understanding of the "big picture", in which the different actors perceived and reacted to the crises and their challenges.

The investigation of the four case studies also showed that the definition and evaluation of a crisis are challenging. To this end several factors play a fundamental role: Not only the temporality *per se*, but more specifically the intersection of the temporalities of the different perspectives, and, in turn, the aysnchronicity that emerges even within the same temporal frame due to different access to different sources. Since our ultimate goal, as historians, is to understand the emic perspective(s) of the ancient cultures as closely as possible, it is important to always remember that in order to do so, it is necessary to eliminate the temporal noise of the message and to stay, as far as possible, in sync with the sources, always remembering that the ancient actors created them not for us, but for themselves, their purposes, their agendas, and in their time.

Bibliography

Alaura, S. 2020. "The Much-Fabled End of the Hittite Empire. Tracing the History of a Crucial Topic", in: S. de Martino / E. Devecchi (eds.), *Anatolia Between the 13th and the 12th century BCE*, Eothen 23, Firenze: LoGisma, 9–30.

Altvater, E. / Mahnkopf, B. 1996. *Grenzen der Globalisierung. Ökonomie, Ökologie und Politik in der Weltgesellschaft*, Münster: Westfälisches Dampfboot.

Alp, S. 1995. "Zur Lage der Stadt Tarḫuntašša", in: O. Carruba / M. Giorgieri / C. Mora (eds.), *Atti del II Congresso Internazionale di Hittitologia. Pavia, 28 giugno – 2 luglio 1993*, Studia Mediterranea 9, Pavia: Iuculano, 1–11.

Archi, A. 1971. "The Propaganda of Ḫattušiliš III", *Studi micenei ed egeo-anatolici* 14, 185–215.

Archi, A. 1997. "Egyptians and Hittites in Contact", in: I. Brancoli / E. Ciampani / A. Roccati / L. Sist (eds.), *L'impero ramesside, Convegno Internazionale in onore di Sergio Donadoni,* Vicino Oriente Quaderno 1, Roma: Dipartimento di Scienze Storiche Archeologiche e Antropologiche dell'Antichità, 1–15.

Archi, A. 2002. "Ittiti e Egiziani: due culture a confronto", in: M. C. Guidotti / F. Pecchioli Daddi (eds.), *La battaglia di Qadesh: Ramesse II contro gli Ittiti per la conquista della Siria*, Livorno: Sillabe, 21–25.

Archi, A. 2003. "Middle Hittite – Middle Kingdom", in: G. Beckman / R. Beal / G. McMahon (eds.), *Hittite Studies in Honor of Harry A. Hoffner Jr. on the Occasion of His 65th Birthday*, Winona Lake: Eisenbrauns, 1–12.

Archi, A. 2005. "Remarks on the Early Empire Documents", *Altorientalische Forschungen* 32, 225–229.

Arroyo, A. forthcoming. "Kurunt(iy)a's Rock Relief of Hatip and His Use of the Title MAGNUS.REX", in: M. Pallavidini / C. Coppini / J. Bach (eds.), *Change, Order, Remembrance. Crisis and Religion in the Ancient Near East. Proceedings of the Workshop held at the 18th EASR Conference, Pisa, August 30th – September 3rd 2021,* Kasion 13, Münster: Zaphon, 21–38.

Astour, M. C. 1989. *Hittite History and Absolute Chronology of the Bronze Age,* Studies in Mediterranean Archaeology and Literature 73, Partille: P. Åström.

Bahar, H., Çay T., İscan, F. 2007. "The Land and City of Tarhuntašša Geodetic Researches around it", in: A. Georgopoulos (ed.), Proceedings of the *XXI International CIPA 2007: AntiCIPAting the Future of the Cultural past: Zappeion Megaron, Athens, Greece, 01-06 October 2007,* ISPRS Archives XXXVI-5/C53, Athens: CIPA, 3 pages.

Beckman, G. 1995. "Royal Ideology and State Administration in Hittite Anatolia", in: J. M. Sasson (ed.), *Civilizations of the Ancient Near East, Volume I,* New York: Scribner, 529–543.

Beckman, G. 1999. *Hittite Diplomatic Texts,* Society of Biblical Literature. Writings from the Ancient World 7, 2nd edition, Atlanta: Scholars Press.

Bittel, K. 1976. *Die Hethiter. Die Kunst Anatoliens vom Ende des 3. bis zum Anfang des 1. Jahrtausends vor Christus,* München: Beck.

Blackbourn, D. 2012. "'The Horologe of Time': Periodization in History", *Publications of the Modern Language Association of America* 127/2, 301–307.

Bloch, M. 1992. *The Historian's Craft* (Translation P. Putnam), Manchester: Manchester University Press.

Braudel, F. 1958. "Histoire et Sciences sociales: La longue durée", *Annales Economie – Societés – Civilisations* 13/4, 725–753.

Breyer, F. 2010. *Ägypten und Anatolien. Politische, kulturelle und sprachliche Kontakte zwischen dem Niltal und Kleinasien im 2. Jahrtausend v. Chr.*, Österreichische Akademie der Wissenschaften.

https://doi.org/10.1515/9783111712383-006

Denkschriften der Gesamtakademie XLIII, Wien: Verlag der Österreichischen Akademie der Wissenschaften.

Bryce, T. 2005. *The Kingdom of the Hittites*, Oxford / New York: Oxford University Press.

Cammarosano, M., Weihrauch, K., Maruhn, F., Jendritzki, G., Kohl, P. L. 2019. "They wrote on Wax. Wax boards in the Ancient Near East", *Mesopotamia* 54, 121–180.

Cancik, H. 1970. *Mythische und historische Wahrheit. Interpretationen zu Texten der hethitischen, biblischen und griechischen Historiographie*, Stuttgarter Bibelstudien 48, Stuttgart: Katholisches Bibelwerk.

Carruba, O. 1976. "Le relazioni fra l'Anatolia e l'Egitto intorno alla metà del II millennio a.C.", *Oriens Antiquus* 15, 295–309.

Cavaignac, E. 1935–1937. "L'Égypte et le Hatti vers 1302", *Mélanges Maspero* 2,2, Mémoires / Institut français d'archéologie orientale du Caire. Ministère de l'instruction Publique et des Beaux-Arts 66, 357–360.

Cordani, V. 2017. *Lettere fra Egiziani e Ittiti*, Testi del Vicino Oriente antico 4.5, Torino: Paideia.

Cornelius, F. 1979. *Geschichte der Hethiter. Mit besonderer Berücksichtigung der geographischen Verhältnisse und der Rechtsgeschichte*, Darmstadt: Wissenschaftliche Buchgesellschaft.

D'Alfonso, L. 2005. *Le procedure giudiziarie ittite in Siria (XIII sec. a. C.)*, Studia Mediterranea 17, Pavia: Italian University Press.

D'Alfonso, L. 2011. "Seeking a Political Space: Thoughts on the Formative Stage of Hittite Administration in Syria", *Altorientalische Forschungen* 38, 163–176.

D'Alfonso, L. 2014. "The Kingdom of Tarhuntassa: A Reassessment of its Timeline and Political Significance", in: P. Taracha / M. Kapełuś (eds.), *Proceedings of the 8th International Congress of Hittitology, Warsaw, September 5–9, 2011*, Warsaw: Agade, 216–235.

D'Alfonso, L. 2020. "An Age of Experimentation: New Thoughts on the Multiple Outcomes Following the Fall of the Hittite Empire After the Results of the Excavations at Niğde-Kınık Höyük (South Cappadocia)", in: S. de Martino / E. Devecchi (eds.), *Anatolia Between the 13th and the 12th Century BCE*, Eothen 23, Firenze: LoGisma, 95–116.

De Martino, S. 1993. "Problemi di cronologia ittita: Una rassegna critica", *La Parola del Passato* 48, 218–240.

De Martino, S. (ed.) 2022. *Handbook Hittite Empire. Power Structures*, Empires through the Ages in Global Perspective 1, Oldenbourg: DeGruyter.

De Martino, S. 2022a. "Hatti: From Regional Polity to Empire", in: S. de Martino (ed.), *Handbook Hittite Empire. Power Structures*, Empires through the Ages in Global Perspective 1, Oldenbourg: DeGruyter, 205–270.

De Martino, S. 2022b. "The Collapse of the Hittite Kingdom", in: M. Gehler / R. Rollinger / P. Strobl (eds.), *The End of Empires*, Wiesbaden: Springer, 81–96.

De Martino, S. 2023. "The Edict Issued by the Hittite King Ḫattušili III Concerning the Priesthood of the Goddess Ištar/Šaušga", in: C. Mora / G. Torri (eds.), *Administrative Practices and Political Control in Anatolian and Syro-Anatolian Polities in the 2nd and 1st Millennium BCE*, Studia Asiana 13, Firenze: Firenze University Press, 9–23.

Del Monte, G. F. 1985. "Muršili II e l'Egitto", in: S. F. Bondì / S. Pernigotti / F. Serra / A. Vivian (eds.), *Studi in onore di Edda Bresciani*, Pisa: Giardini, 161–167.

Del Monte, G. F. 2009. *L'opera storiografica di Mursili II re di Hattusa, Vol. I: Le gesta di Suppiluliuma*, Pisa: Pisa University Press.

Devecchi, E. 2012. "Aziru, Servant of Three Masters?", *Altorientalische Forschungen* 39, 38–48.

Devecchi, E. 2015. *Trattati internazionali ittiti*, Brescia: Paideia.

Devecchi, E. / Miller, J. L. 2011. "Hittite-Egyptian Synchronisms and their Consequences for Ancient Near Eastern Chronology", in: J. Mynářová (ed.), *Egypt and the Near East – the Crossroads. Proceedings of an International Conference on the Relations of Egypt and the Near East in the Bronze Age, Prague, September 1–3, 2010*, Prague: Czech Institute of Egyptology, 139–176.

De Vos, J. 2007. "Les relations égypto-hittites: Apologie d'un retour aux sources de la diplomatie antique", *Bulletin de la Societas Anatolica* 1, 41–47.

Diamond, J. 2005. *Collapse: How Societies Choose to Fail or Succeed*, New York: Viking Penguin.

Dinçol, A. M., Yakar, Y., Dinçol, B., Taffet, A. 2000. "The Borders of the Appanage Kingdom of Tarhuntašša - A Geographical and Archaeological Assessment", *Anatolica* 26, 1–29.

Dinçol, A. M., Yakar, Y., Dinçol, B., Taffet, A. 2001. "Die Grenzen von Tarhuntašša im Lichte geographischer Beobachtungen", in: E. Jean / A. M. Dinçol / S. Durugönül (eds.), *La Cilicie: Espaces et Pouvoirs Locaux (2e millénaire av. J.-C. – 4e siècle ap. J.-C.), Actes de la Table ronde internationale d'Istanbul, 2–5 novembre 1999*, Varia Anatolica XIII, Istanbul / Paris: IFEA, 79–86.

Doğan-Alparslan, M. 2012. *"Hitit Kralı II. Muwatalli: Kişiliği ve İcraatı. Filolojik Belgeler Işığında / Der hethitische König Muwatalli II: Sein Charakter und seine Mannestaten (Im Licht der philologischen Belege), Studia ad Orientem Antiquum / Eski Doğu Araştırmaları* 1, Istanbul: Ege Yayınları.

Edel, E. 1994. *Die ägyptisch-hethitische Korrespondenz aus Boghazköi in babylonischer und hethitischer Sprache*, Abhandlungen der Rheinisch-westfälischen Akademie der Wissenschaften 77, Opladen: Westdeutscher Verlag.

Edel, E. 1997. *Der Vertrag zwischen Ramses II. von Ägypten und Hattušili III. von Hatti*, Wissenschaftliche Veröffentlichungen der Deutschen Orient-Gesellschaft 95, Berlin: Gebr. Mann.

Faulseit, R. K. (ed.). 2016. *Beyond Collapse: Archaeological Perspectives on Resilience, Revitalization, and Transformation in Complex Societies*, Carbondale: Southern Illinois University Press.

Floridi, L. 2002. "Infosphère, une définition", *Boson2x*, 20 December 2002.

Forlanini, M. 2017. "South Central: The Lower Land and Tarḫuntašša", in: M. Weeden / L. Z. Ullmann (eds.), *Hittite Landscape and Geography*, Handbuch der Orientalistik 121, Leiden / Boston: Brill, 239–252.

Forrer, E. 1926. *Die Boghazköi-Texte in Umschrift, 2. Bd.: Geschichtliche Texte aus dem alten und neuen Chatti-Reich*, Wissenschaftliche Veröffentlichungen der Deutschen Orient-Gesellschaft 42, Leipzig: J. C. Hinrichs'sche Buchhandlung.

Freu, J. 1987. "Problèmes de chronologie et de géographie hittites. Madduwatta et les débuts de l'empire", *Hethitica* 8, 123–175.

Freu, J. 2002. "La chronologie du règne de Suppiluliuma: Essai de mise au point", in: P. Taracha (ed.), *Silva Anatolica. Anatolian Studies Presented to Maciej Popko on the Occasion of His 65th Birthday*, Warsaw: Agade, 87–107.

Gehler, M., Rollinger, R., Stroble, P. 2002. "Decline, Erosion, Implosion and Fall, or Just Transformation? Diverging Ends of Empires Through Time and Space, in: M. Gehler / R. Rollinger / P. Strobl (eds.), *The End of Empires*, Wiesbaden: Springer, 1–45.

Gerçek, N. İ. 2017. "Approaches to Hittite Imperialism: A View from the "Old Kingdom" and "Early Empire" Periods (c. 1650-1350 BCE)", in: A. Schachner (ed.), *Innovation versus Beharrung: Was macht den Unterschied des hethitischen Reichs im Anatolien des 2. Jahrtausends v. Chr.*, Byzas 23, Istanbul: Yayınları, 21–38.

Gilan, A. 2005. "Die hethitischen 'Mannestaten' und ihre Adressaten", in: A. Süel (ed.), *V. Uluslararası Hititoloji Kongresi Bildirileri, Çorum 02-08 Eylül 2002 – Acts of the Vth International Congress of Hittitology, Çorum September 02-08, 2002*, Ankara: Nokta Ofset, 359–369.

Gilan, A. 2015. *Formen und Inhalte althethitischer historischer Literatur,* Texte der Hethiter 29, Heidelberg: Winter.

Gilan, A. 2022. "'Šawoška of Šamuḫa, My Lady, caught him like a fish with a net': Usurping the Throne and writing about it", in: L. Portuese / M. Pallavidini (eds.), *Ancient Near Eastern Weltanschauungen in Contact and in Contrast. Rethinking Ideology and Propaganda in the Ancient Near East*, (wEdge 2) Münster: Zaphon, 289–308.

Giorgieri, M. 2020. "The Dynastic Crisis of the Hittite Royal Family in the Late Empire Period: Evidence from the Loyalty Oaths", in: S. de Martino / E. Devecchi (eds.), *Anatolia Between the 13th and the 12th century BCE*, Eothen 23, Firenze: LoGisma, 155–175.

Giusfredi, F., Pisaniello, V., Matessi, A. (eds.) 2023. *Contacts of Languages and Peoples in the Hittite and Post-Hittite World,f Volume 1: The Bronze Age and Hatti*, Ancient Languages and Civilizations 4, Leiden: Brill.

Goedegebuure, P. 2006a. "Hittite Historical Texts I: "The Bilingual Testament of Hattusili I"", in: M. W. Chavalas (ed.), *The Ancient Near East: Historical Sources in Translation*, Malden / Oxford / Victoria: Blackwell, 222–228.

Goedegebuure, P. 2006b. "Hittite Historical Texts I: "The proclamation of Telipinu", in: M. W. Chavalas (ed.), *The Ancient Near East: Historical Sources in Translation*, Malden / Oxford / Victoria: Blackwell, 228–235.

Götze, A. 1928. *Das Hethiter-Reich. Seine Stellung zwischen Ost und West*, Der Alte Orient 27/2, Leipzig: Hinrichs'sche Buchhandlung.

Götze, A. 1968. "The Predecessors of Šuppiluliumaš of Ḫatti and the Chronology of the Ancient Near East", *Journal of Cuneiform Studies* 22, 46–50.

Guidotti, M. C., Pecchioli Daddi, F. (eds.), 2002. *La battaglia di Qadesh: Ramesse II contro gli Ittiti per la conquista della Siria*, Livorno: Sillabe.

Green, W. A. 1995. "Periodizing World History", *History and Theory* 34, 99–111.

Gurney, O. R. 1952. *The Hittites. A Summary of the Art, Achievements, and Social Organization of a Great People of Asia Minor during the 2nd Millennium B.C. as Discovered by Modern Excavators*, London: Pelican Book.

Gurney, O. R. 1974. "The Hittite Line of Kings and Chronology", in: K. Bittel / Ph. H. J. Houwink ten Cate / E. Reiner (eds.), *Anatolian Studies Presented to Hans Gustav Güterbock on the Occasion of his 65th Birthday*, Publications de l'Institut Historique-Archéologique Néerlandais de Stamboul 35, Leiden: Nederlands Instituut voor het Nabije Oosten, 105–111.

Gurvitch, G. 1958. *La multiplicité de temps sociaux*, Paris: Centre de Documentation Universitaire.

Güterbock H. G., 1956. "The Deeds of Suppiluliuma as Told by His Son, Mursili II", *Journal of Cuneiform Studies* 10, 41–68, 75–98, 107–130.

Haas, V. 2006. *Die hethitische Literatur. Texte, Stilistik, Motive*, Berlin / New York: De Gruyter.

Haas, V. 2006. *Die hethitische Literatur. Texte, Stilistik, Motive*, Berlin / New York: De Gruyter.

Heltzer, M. 1977. "The Metal Trade of Ugarit and the Problem of Transportation of Commercial Goods", *Iraq* 39, 203–211.

Hoffmann, I. 1984. *Der Erlass Telipinus*, Texte der Hethiter 11, Heidelberg: Winter.

Hoffner, H. A. 1975. "Propaganda and Political Justification in Hittite Historiography", in: H. Goedicke / J. J. M. Roberts (eds.), *Unity and Diversity. Essays in the History, Literature, and Religion of the Ancient Near East*, Baltimore / London: Johns Hopkins University Press, 49–62.

Hoffner, H. A. 1980. "Histories and Historians of the Ancient Near East: The Hittites", *Orientalia Nova Series* 49, 283–332.

Hoffner, H. A. 1992. "The Last Days of Khattusha", in: W. A. Ward / M. Sharp Joukowsky (eds.), *The Crisis Years: The 12th Century B.C. from Beyond the Danube to the Tigris*, Dubuque: Kendall / Hunt, 46–52.

Hoffner, H. A. 2003a. "Hittite Archival Documents, Letters: 2. Later New Kingdom (Hattušili III to Suppiluliuma II) (ca. 1250–1180 BCE)", in: W. W. Hallo / K. L. Younger Jr. (eds.), *The Context of Scripture, Vol. III: Archival Documents from the Biblical World*, Leiden / Boston: Brill, 51–53.

Hoffner, H. A. 2003b. "Hittite Canonical Compositions, 2. Historiography, The Hittite Conquest of Cyprus: Two Inscriptions of Suppiluliuma II", in: W. W. Hallo / K. L. Younger Jr. (eds.), *The Context of Scripture, Vol. I: Canonical Compositions from the Biblical World*, Leiden / Boston: Brill, 182–193.

Houwink ten Cate, Ph. H. J. 1974. "The Early and Late Phases of Urhi-Tesub's Career", in: K. Bittel / Ph. H. J. Houwink ten Cate / E. Reiner (eds.), *Anatolian Studies Presented to Hans Gustav Güterbock on the Occasion of his 65th Birthday*, Publications de l'Institut Historique-Archéologique Néerlandais de Stamboul 35, Leiden: Nederlands Instituut voor het Nabije Oosten, 123–150.

Houwink ten Cate, Ph. H. J. 1994. "Urhi-Tessub revisited", *Bibliotheca Orientalis* 51, 233–259.

Imparati, F. 1988. "Interventi di politica economica dei sovrani ittiti e stabilità del potere", in: A. Shafik / A. Zanardo (eds.), *Stato, Economia, Lavoro nel Vicino Oriente antico. Istituto Gramsci Toscano. Scritti del Seminario di Orientalistica antica*, Milano: FrancoAngeli, 225–239.

Imparati, F. 1995. "Apology of Ḫattušili III or Designation of his Successor?", in: Th. P. J. van den Hout / J. de Roos (eds.), *Studio Historiae Ardens. Ancient Near Eastern Studies Presented to Philo H. J. Houwink ten Cate on the Occasion of his 65th Birthday*, Publications de l'Institut Historique-Archéologique Néerlandais de Stamboul 74, Leiden: Nederlands Instituut voor het Nabije Oosten, 143–157.

Jordheim, H. 2014. "1. Introduction: Multiple Times and the Work of Synchronization", *History and Theory* 53/4, 498–518.

Jordheim, H. 2017. "Synchronizing the World: Synchronism as Historiographical Practice, Then and Now", *History of the Present* 7/1, 59–95.

Kitchen, K. A. 1996. *Ramesside Inscriptions Translated and Annotated. Translations, Vol. II: Ramesses II, Royal Inscriptions*, Oxford: Blackwell.

Klengel, H. 1974. "'Hungerjahre' In Ḫatti", *Altorientalische Forschungen* 1, 165–174.

Klengel, H. 1999. *Geschichte des hethitischen Reiches*, Handbuch der Orientalistik 34, Leiden / Boston / Köln: Brill.

Klinger, J. 1995. "Synchronismen in der Epoche vor Šuppiluliuma I. - einige Anmerkungen zur Chronologie der mittelhethitischen Geschichte", in: M. Giorgieri / O. Carruba (eds.), *Atti del II Congresso Internazionale di Hittitologia. Pavia 28 giugno – 2 luglio 1993*, Studia Mediterranea 9, Pavia: Iuculano, 235–248.

Klinger, J. 2022. "Zu den Anfängen der hethitischen Überlieferung überhaupt und zur Methode der paläographischen Textdatierung", in: E. Cancik-Kirschbaum / I. Schrakamp (eds.), *Transfer, Adaption und Neukonfigurierung von Schrift- und Sprachwissen im Alten Orient*, Episteme in Bewegung. Beiträge zu einer transdisziplinären Wissensgeschichte 25, Wiesbaden: Harrassowitz, 255–340.

Knapp, A. 2015. *Royal Apologetic in the Ancient Near East*,Writings from the Ancient World Supplement Series 4, Atlanta: SBL Press.

Koselleck, R. 2000. *Zeitschichten. Studien zur Historik.* Frankfurt am Main: Suhrkamp.

Koselleck, R. 2006. "Crisis", *Journal of the History of Ideas* 67/2, 357–400.

Laroche, E. 1955. "Chronologie hittite: État des questions", *Anadolu* 2, 1–22.

Laroche, E. 1971. *Catalogue des textes hittites*, Études et commentaires 75, Paris: Klincksieck.

Le Goff, J. 1992. *History and Memory*, New York: Columbia University Press.

Liverani, M. 1974. "Memorandum on the Approach to Historiographic Texts." *Orientalia* 42, 178–194.

Liverani, M. 1977. "Storiografia politica hittita. II. Telepinu, ovvero: della solidarietà", *Oriens Antiquus* 16, 105–131.

Liverani, M. 1990. "Hattushili alle prese con la propaganda ramesside", M. Marazzi / G. Wilhelm (eds.), *Gedenkschrift Einar von Schuler (28. 10. 1930 - 15. 2. 1990), Orientalia Nova Series* 59/2, 207–217.

Liverani, M. 1994. *Guerra e diplomazia nell'antico Oriente: 1600–1100 a.C.*, Bari: Laterza.

Liverani, M. 2000. "The Great Powers' Club", in: R. Cohen / R. Westbrook (eds.), *Amarna Diplomacy. The Beginnings of International Relations*, Baltimore / London: Johns Hopkins University Press, 15–27.

Liverani, M. 2001. *International Relations in the Ancient Near East, 1600–1100 BC*, New York: Palgrave.

Liverani, M. 2002. "La battaglia di Qadesh", in: M. C. Guidotti / F. Pecchioli Daddi (eds.), 2002. *La battaglia di Qadesh: Ramesse II contro gli Ittiti per la conquista della Siria*, Livorno: Sillabe, 17–20.

Liverani, M. 2013. *The Ancient Near East. History, Society and Economy*, London / New York: Routledge.

Lorenz, C. 2017. "'The Times They Are a-Changin'. On Time, Space and Periodization in History", in: M. Carretero / S. Berger / M. Grever (eds.), Palgrave Handbook of Research in Historical Culture and Education, London: Palgrave Macmillan, 109–131.

Lucas, G. 2005. *The Archaeology of Time*, London: Routledge.

Manuelli, F. 2016. "What Remains when Contact Breaks Off? Survival of Knowledge and Techniques in the Material Culture of the Peripheral Regions of the Hittite Empire after Its Dissolution", in: E. Foietta / C. Ferrandi / E. Quirico / F. Giusto / M. Mortarini / J. Bruno / L. Somma (eds.), *Cultural & Material Contacts in the Ancient Near East. Proceedings of the International Workshop 1–2 December 2014, Torino*, Sesto Fiorentino: Apice Libri, 26–35.

Marazzi, M. 1994. "Ma gli hittiti scrivevano veramente su 'legno'?", in: P. Cipriano / P. Di Giovine / M. Mancini (eds.), *Miscellanea di studi linguistici in onore di Walter Belardi*, Linguistica indoeuropea e non indoeuropea I, Rome: Il calamo, 131–60

Meissner, B. 1918. "Die Beziehungen Ägyptens zum Ḫattireiche nach ḫattischen Quellen", *Zeitschrift der Deutschen Morgenländischen Gesellschaft* 72, 32–64.

Melchert, H. C. 2007. "The Borders of Tarhuntassa Revisited", in: M. Alparslan / M. Doğan-Alparslan / H. Peker (eds.), *VITA. Festschrift in Honor of Belkıs Dinçol and Ali Dinçol*, Istanbul: Ege Yayınları, 507–513.

Michalowski, P. 2015. "Literacy in the Ancient Near East", in: R. S. Bagnall / K. Brodersen / C. Champion / A. Erskine / S. Huebner (eds.), *The Encyclopaedia of Ancient History*, https://doi.org/10.1002/9781444338386.wbeah26301.

Middleton, G. D. 2017. *Understanding Collapse. Ancient History and Modern Myths*, Cambridge: Cambridge University Press.

Miller, J. L. 2007. "Amarna Age Chronology and the Identity of Nibḫururiya in the Light of a Newly Reconstructed Hittite Text", *Altorientalische Forschungen* 34, 252–293.

Miller, J. L. 2020. "Are There Signs of the Decline of the Late Hittite State in the Textual Documentation from Hattuša?", in: S. de Martino / E. Devecchi (eds.), *Anatolia Between the 13th and the 12th century BCE*, Eothen 23, Firenze: LoGisma, 237–255.

Mora, C. 2008. "La 'Parola del re'. Testi ittiti a carattere politico-giuridico e politico-amministrativo: editti e istruzioni", in: M. Liverani / C. Mora (eds.), *I diritti nel mondo cuneiforme (Mesopotamia e regioni adiacenti, ca. 2500–500 a.C.)*, Pavia: IUSS Press, 293–323.

Mora, C., Giorgieri, M. 2004. *Le Lettere Tra I Re Ittiti e I Re Assiri Ritrovate a Ḫattuša*, History of the Ancient Near East. Monographs VII, Padova: Sargon.

Moran, W. L. 1992. *The Amarna Letters. Edited and Translated*, Baltimore / London: Johns Hopkins University Press.

Murnane, W. J. 1990. *The Road to Kadesh. A Historical Interpretation of the Battle Reliefs of King Sety I at Karnak*, second edition revised, Studies in Ancient Oriental Civilization 42, Chicago: Oriental Institute.

Mynářová, J. 2007. *Language of Amarna – Language of Diplomacy. Perspectives on the Amarna Letters*, Prague: Charles University.

Planelles Orozco, A. 2017 "The Hittite Title *Tuhkanti* Revisited: Towards a Precise Characterisation of the Office", *Anatolian Studies* 67, 109–127.

Otten, H. 1951. "Die hethitischen "Königslisten" und die altorientalische Chronologie", *Mitteilung der Deutschen Orient-Gesellschaft* 83, 47–71.

Otten, H. 1981. *Die Apologie Hattusilis III. Das Bild der Überlieferung*, Studien zu den Boğazköy-Texten 24, Wiesbaden: Harrassowitz.

Otten, H. 1988. *Die Bronzetafel aus Boğazköy. Ein Staatsvertrag Tutḫalijas IV.*, Studien zu den Boğazköy-Texten Beiheft 1, Wiesbaden: Harrassowitz.

Pallavidini, M. 2016a. *Diplomazia e propaganda in epoca imperiale ittita. Forma e prassi*, Dresdner Beiträge zur Hethitologie 48, Wiesbaden: Harrassowitz.

Pallavidini, M. 2016b. "Les dispositions internationales des rois hittites trouvées à Ougarit. Décrets ou jugements? Une proposition de classification", *Res Antiquae* 13, 219–234.

Pallavidini, M. 2017a. "Ḫakpiš, la prima "Sekundogenitur" di Ḫatti? Considerazioni sul rapporto giuridico di Ḫattušili con Muwatalli e Urḫi-Teššup sulla base di CTH 81", *Res Antiquae* 14, 205–220.

Pallavidini, M. 2017b. "The Treaties of Šuppiluliuma II: The Norm and Innovation of the Treaty as Juridical Medium", *Rosetta Journal* 19, 1–19.

Pallavidini, M. forthcoming. Religion and Politics in the Hittite Empire: A Crisis and its Perception in the "Apology" of Ḫattušili III", in: M. Pallavidini / C. Coppini / J. Bach (eds.), *Change, Order, Remembrance Crisis and Religion in the Ancient Near East. Proceedings of the Workshop Held at the 18th EASR Conference Pisa, August 30th – September 3rd 2021*, Kasion 13, Münster: Zaphon, 39–56.

Pintore, F. 1978. *Il matrimonio interdinastico nel Vicino Oriente durante i secoli XV – XIII*, Orientis Antiqui Collectio XIV, Roma: Ipocan.

Rüsen, J. 2013. *Historik. Theorie der Geschichtswissenschaft*. Köln / Weimar / Wien: Böhlau Verlag.

Rüsen, J. 2020. *Historische Sinnbildung. Grundlagen, Formen, Entwicklungen*. Wiesbaden: Springer.

Rüster, Ch. / Wilhelm, G. 2012. *Landschenkungsurkunden hethitischer Könige*, Studien zu den Boğazköy-Texten Beiheft 4, Wiesbaden: Harrassowitz.

Schwemer, D. 2006a. "Tukultī-Ninurta I. von Assur(?) an Ibiranu von Ugarit(?): Der hethitisch-assyrische Krieg zu Zeiten Tutḫalijas IV. (RS 34.165)", *Texte aus der Umwelt des Alten Testaments. Neue Folge* 3, 254–256.

Schwemer, D. 2006b. "Ein hethitischer Prinz(?) an ʿAmmurāpi von Ugarit(?): Getreidelieferungen wegen einer Hungersnot in Anatolien (RS 20.212)", *Texte aus der Umwelt des Alten Testaments. Neue Folge* 3, 258–260.

Seeher, J. 2001. "Die Zerstörung der Stadt Ḫattuša", in: G. Wilhelm (ed.), *Akten des IV. Internationalen Kongresses für Hethitologie, Würzburg, 4.–8. Oktober 1999*, Studien zu den Boğazköy-Texten 45, Wiesbaden: Harrassowitz, 623–634.

Seeher, J. 2010. "After the Empire: Observations on the Early Iron Age in Central Anatolia", in: I. Singer (ed.), *Ipamati kistamati pari tumatimis: Luwian and Hittite Studies Presented to J. David Hawkins on the Occasion of his 70th Birthday*, Tel Aviv: Institute of Archaeology, 220–229.

Sethe, K. 1926. "Neue Forschungen zu den Beziehungen zwischen Ägypten und dem Chattireiche auf Grund ägyptischer Quellen", *Deutsche Literaturzeitung für Kritik der internationalen Wissenschaft* 47, 1875–1880.

Singer, I. 1985. "The Battle of Niḫriya and the End of the Hittite Empire", *Zeitschrift für Assyriologie und Vorderasiatische Archäologie* 75, 100–123.

Singer, I. 2000. "New Evidence on the End of the Hittite Empire", in: E. O. Oren (ed.), *The Sea Peoples and Their World. A Reassessment*, Philadelphia: University of Pennsylvania Press, 21–34.

Singer, I. 2002. *Hittite Prayers*, SBL Writings from the Ancient World 11, Atlanta: Society of Biblical Literature.

Singer, I. 2004. "The Kuruštama Treaty Revisited", in: D. Groddek / S. Rößle (eds.), *Šarnikzel. Hethitologische Studien zum Gedenken an Emil Orgetorix Forrer*, Dresdner Beiträge zur Hethitologie 10, Dresden: Technische Universität, 591–607.

Singer, I. 2006. "The Failed Reforms of Akhenaten and Muwatalli", *British Museum Studies in Ancient Egypt and Sudan* 6, 37–58.

Stavi, B. 2011. "The Genealogy of Suppiluliuma I", *Altorientalische Forschungen* 38, 226–239.

Stavi, B. 2015. *The Reign of Tudhaliya II and Šuppiluliuma I. The Contribution of the Hittite Documentation to a Reconstruction of the Amarna Age*, Texte der Hethiter 31, Heidelberg: Winter Universitätsverlag.

Sturtevant, E. H. / Bechtel, G. 1935. *A Hittite Chrestomathy*, William Dwight Whitney Linguistic Series, Philadelphia: Linguistic Society of America University of Pennsylvania.

Sürenhagen, D. 1992. "Untersuchungen zur Bronzetafel und weiteren Verträgen mit der Sekundogenitur in Tarḫuntašša", *Orientalistische Literaturzeitung* 87, 341–371.

Ünal, A. 1974. *Ḫattušili III. Teil 1: Ḫattušili bis zu seiner Thronbesteigung, Band 1: Historischer Abriß*, Texte der Hethiter 3, Heidelberg: Winter.

Van den Hout, Th. P. J. 1995. *Der Ulmitešub-Vertrag. Eine prosopographische Untersuchung*, Studien zu den Boğazköy-Texten 38, Wiesbaden: Harrassowitz.

Van den Hout, Th. 2003. "Hittite Canonical Composition, 3. Biography and Autobiography, The Proclamation of Telipinu", in: W. W. Hallo / K. L. Younger Jr. (eds.), *The Context of Scripture, Vol. I: Canonical Compositions from the Biblical World*, Leiden / Boston: Brill, 194–198.

Van den Hout, Th. 2006. "Hittite Historical Texts II: Muršili II's 'Second' Plague Prayer", in: M. W. Chavalas (ed.), *The Ancient Near East: Historical Sources in Translation*, Malden / Oxford / Victoria: Blackwell, 263–266.

Van den Hout, Th. 2021. *A History of Hittite Literacy. Writing and Reading in Late Bronze-Age Anatolia (1650–1200 BC)*, Cambridge: Cambridge University Press.

Waal, W. 2011. "They Wrote on Wood. The Case for a Hieroglyphic Scribal Tradition on Wooden Writing Boards in Hittite Anatolia", *Anatolian Studies* 61, 21–34.

Wilhelm, G. 1991. "Probleme der hethitischen Chronologie", *Orientalistische Literaturzeitung* 86, 469–476.

Wilhelm, G. / Boese, J. 1987. "Absolute Chronologie und die hethitische Geschichte des 15. und 14. Jahrhunderts v.Chr.", in: P. Åström (ed.), *High, Middle or Low? Acts of an International Colloquium on Absolute Chronology Held at the University of Gothenburg 20th–22nd August 1987. Parts 1–2*, Studies in Mediterranean Archaeology and Literature 56–57, Gothenburg, 74–117.

Yakar, J., Dinçol, A. M., Dinçol, B., Taffet, A. 2001. "The Territory of the Appanage Kingdom of Tarḫuntašša - An Archaeological Appraisal", in: G. Wilhelm (ed.), *Akten des IV. Internationalen Kongresses für Hethitologie, Würzburg, 4.–8. Oktober 1999*, Studien zu den Boğazköy-Texten 45, Wiesbaden: Harrassowitz, 711–720.

Zaccagnini, C. 1973. *Lo scambio dei doni nel Vicino Oriente durante i secoli XV – XIII*, Oriens Antiqui Collectio 11, Roma: Centro per le Antichità e la Storia dell'Arte del Vicino Oriente.

Zaccagnini, C. 1990. "The Forms of Alliance and Subjugation in the Near East of the Late Bronze Age", in: L. Canfora / M. Liverani / C. Zaccagnini (eds.), *I trattati nel mondo antico. Forma, ideologia, funzione*, Roma: L'erma di Bretschneider, 37–79.

Indices

Personal, Divine, and Royal Names

Alluwamna 8
Ammuna 8
Arma-Tarḫunta 27, 40, 42
Arnuwanda I 8
Arnuwanda II 8
Arnuwanda III 8
Aziru 33, 52

Bentešina 39 f., 46

Ḫakpiš 35
Ḫantili I 8, 19
Ḫantili II 8
Ḫattušaziti 30
Ḫattušili I 8, 19, 21, 24
Ḫattušili III 8, 13, 15, 21–24, 26 f., 34, 37–40, 42–44, 46, 51, 55, 58–61
Ḫuzziya (I) 8
Ḫuzziya II 8

Ibiranu 52 f.
Ištar 38, 41 f., 45

Kadašman-Enlil 40, 43, 45
Kadašman-Turgu 40
Karkemish 45
Kurunta 7, 40, 45 f.

Labarna 8, 19, 21

Mittanamuwa 41, 43
Muršili I 8, 19, 24
Muršili II 8, 30, 33, 36, 40
Muršili III 8, 26
Muwatalli I 8
Muwatalli II 8, 22, 26, 35, 40, 45

Nerikkaili 40, 44
Nibḫururiya 30

Piḫawalwi 52
Pirwa 41

Ramesses 25–29, 33–36, 38–40, 43
Rib-Addu 53

Šipa-Ziti 42
Šuppiluliuma I 8 f., 12–14, 24, 31, 33, 36, 40
Šuppiluliuma II 8 f., 48 f., 53–55

Taḫurwaili 8
Telipinu 8, 11–13, 15, 17–24, 54, 59 f.
Tukultī-Ninurta I 53
Tutḫaliya III 8
Tutḫaliya I/II 8
Tutḫaliya IV 7 f., 26, 39 f., 43, 46, 51

Urḫi-Teššup 8, 22, 26, 34, 37 f., 40–47, 61

Zannanza 30, 33
Zidanta I 8
Zidanta II 8

Geographical Names

Alluwamna 8
Ammuna 8
Arma-Tarḫunta 27, 40, 42
Arnuwanda I 8
Arnuwanda II 8
Arnuwanda III 8
Aziru 33, 52

Bentešina 39 f., 46

Texts

Deeds of Šuppiluliuma *See* CTH 40

EA 41 31
EA 42 31
EA 43 31
EA 44 31

KBo 1.10+ 40, 43, 46
KBo 1.15++ 27
KBo 1.24+ 43
KBo 5.6 30
KBo 6.29+ 41 f.
KBo 12.38 53 f.
KUB 3.22+ 43
KUB 3.71 40
KUB 21.17 27

Papyrus Chester Beatty III 28
Papyrus Raifé / Sallier III 28
Proclamation of Telipinu *See* CTH 19

RS 17.133 39
RS 17.229 39
RS 17.238 39
RS 17.247 52
RS 18.114 39
RS 20.212 52
RS 34.165 53 f.

Second Plague Prayer *See* CTH 378.2

Testament of Ḫattušili I *See* CTH 6

www.ingramcontent.com/pod-product-compliance
Lightning Source LLC
Chambersburg PA
CBHW051544230426
43669CB00015B/2716
* 9 7 8 3 1 1 1 7 1 2 1 2 3 *